# With Grit and a Big Heart

# With Grit and a Big Heart

## A Beginner's Guide to Teaching

Theodore G. Zervas

ROWMAN & LITTLEFIELD
*Lanham • Boulder • New York • London*

Published by Rowman & Littlefield
An imprint of The Rowman & Littlefield Publishing Group, Inc.
4501 Forbes Boulevard, Suite 200, Lanham, Maryland 20706
www.rowman.com

86-90 Paul Street, London EC2A 4NE, United Kingdom

British Library Cataloguing in Publication Information Available

**Library of Congress Cataloging-in-Publication Data**

Names: Zervas, Theodore G., author.
Title: With grit and a big heart : a beginner's guide to teaching / Theodore G. Zervas.
Description: Lanham, Maryland : Rowman & Littlefield, [2022] | Includes
    bibliographical references and index. | Summary: "This book is about the teaching
    profession and what it takes to become a successful teacher"—Provided by publisher.
Identifiers: LCCN 2022005534 (print) | LCCN 2022005535 (ebook) | ISBN
    9781475865851 (Cloth : acid-free paper) | ISBN 9781475865868
    (Paperback : acid-free paper) | ISBN 9781475865875 (ePub)
Subjects: LCSH: Teaching—Vocational guidance. | Teachers—Training of.
Classification: LCC LB1775 .Z49 2022 (print) | LCC LB1775 (ebook) |
    DDC 370.71/1—dc23/eng/20220217
LC record available at https://lccn.loc.gov/2022005534
LC ebook record available at https://lccn.loc.gov/2022005535

♾TM The paper used in this publication meets the minimum requirements of American
National Standard for Information Sciences—Permanence of Paper for Printed Library
Materials, ANSI/NISO Z39.48-1992.

*For My Students
and yes, teaching is an art.*

# Contents

# Preface

## What the UEFA Soccer Tournament and Teaching Have in Common

In the summer of 2004, I was on my summer break from teaching high schoolers. I planned to stay in Chicago that summer to watch the UEFA Soccer tournament. As a Greek American, I felt obliged to cheer for the Greek team, even though I knew that they had almost no chance of winning. Nevertheless, family and friends all gathered at my house to cheer for the Greek team.

If you grew up watching international soccer, you know that the best teams have a unique style of playing. Often this reflects their national culture. Brazilians, for example, play like musicians, Spanish like flamenco dancers, Germans like engineers, and Italians like cautious cats. Before 2004, Greece had yet to develop its own style of soccer. But a new coach from Germany named Otto Rehhagel would help Greece find it.

Unlike the other teams in the tournament, Greece did not have big-name talents as Portugal's Cristiano Ronaldo, England's Wayne Rooney, Italy's Gianluigi Buffon, and France's Zinedine Zidane. Antonios Nikopolidis, Theodoros Zagorakis, Angelos Charisteas, and Zisis Vryzas were among those that played for Greece. They were virtually unknown outside of Greece. Otto Rehhagel, however, had come up with a simple yet effective way to win, defend at all costs, frustrate your opponent, and then at the right moment attack. It was an adaptation of an Italian style of soccer called the Catennacio, with Greece in a 2-4-4 defensive formation.

Upon reflecting on the tournament years later, Rehhagel said, "Our opponents were certainly technically better than us, . . . But they have to score their own goals . . . later on they only operated with long balls and looked helpless." What Rehhagel was saying was that when a team resorted to long balls, it was a sign of frustration and desperation, much like a quarterback throwing Hail Mary's the entire game. "It's ok, let them come to us," Rehhagel told his players.

When the tournament began in July, Greece beat Portugal, the tournament favorite. Later, Greece tied Spain and lost to Russia. Greece barely squeezed by to the next round of the tournament. By this time, observers of the tournament noticed Greece. They weren't the most exciting to watch, but they were effective. "Defense! Defense!" Yelled Rehhagel from the sidelines. When that rare opportunity occurred, Rehhagel yelled, "Push forward." Once Greece scored, Rehhagel yelled for his players to fall back on defense.

When Greece was scheduled to face France, the reigning UEFA and World Cup champions in the semifinals, many thought that Greece's run would come to an end. But Rehhagel went ahead and had his players stick to his strategy.

Controlling the midfield for France was Zinedine Zidane, *futboller par exelance* and one of the greatest players to ever play the game of soccer. The game was mostly prosaic in the first half. France was controlling the ball within their midfield, missing some good opportunities and controlling the ball for most of the game. Greece, on the other hand, barely got a shot on goal, but their defense was still standing strong. At 45th minute, the referee blew his whistle to signal the end of the first half and both teams went back to their locker rooms to rest and talk.

After half-time, the players returned for another 45-plus minutes of play. For the first 10 minutes it seemed like the game would look much like it did the first half. But about 11 minutes into the half, an observant eye could see the frustration on the French players' faces. As soon as Rehhagel saw this, he called for his players to attack. Greece began to push forward. Greece's defense moved up, as did the Greek midfield, and all the Greek players began to spread out on the field.

When France had the ball, they could barely get it passed the midfield. Greece had forced France to fall back on defense. At about 57th minute, Angelos Basinas of Greece took possession of the ball just beyond the midfield line. Basinas passed the ball to Theodoros Zagorakis who, haring down the right flank, skillfully flicked the ball above the head of one of the French defenders and then sent the ball over a measured cross toward the twenty-three-year-old Angelos Charisteas. Charisteas headed the ball near the penalty marker, for a textbook precision goal into the left corner of the net. It was a beautifully executed play by Basinas and Zagorakis, and Charisteas's goal wasn't bad either.

The stadium roared. Afterward, Greece fell back on defense. The Greek players all settled calmly behind the midfield line. France had the ball for over 85 percent of the remaining minutes of the game but struggled to score. "Bring on Brazil! Bring on France! Italy! Argentina! Germany! And any other wankers out there!" cheered the Greece fans after the game.

Greece's win against France was its greatest soccer victory in history. But Greece had more games to play. Greece would make it to the final after beating a talented Czech team in overtime with a corner kick that would be headed brilliantly into the Czech net by the veteran Greek player Trianos Dellas.

The tournament final was on July 4, between Greece and Portugal. The two teams had already played each other at the beginning of the tournament. Greece won that meeting 2-1, but Portugal was determined to beat Greece this time.

The first half looked a lot like the Greece-France game, with Portugal having control of the ball most of the half. The Greek players stayed calm and defended. Half-time came and the teams went back to their locker rooms to rest before the second half started.

Once the second half began, things looked quiet. Greece's defense stayed strong while Portugal tried several times to score. By the 12th minute, things began to change. Greece got ready to make a corner kick. Both teams hurried to get into position before Greece's Angelos Basinas shot the ball. Basinas quickly ran to the corner, lined the ball next to the flag, took a few steps back, waited a few seconds, and shot the ball into the air toward the goalie's box.

What happened next seemed like the world was moving in slow motion. When Angelos Charisteas noticed the ball coming toward him, he leaped above one of the Portugal defenders and headed the ball squarely into the back of the net. The Portugal goalie barely moved. The Greece fans roared. As usual, Greece fell back on defense. Portugal went on offense and moved to break through an impervious Greek defense.

Portugal tried time and time again to score but couldn't. Time was quickly running out. At about the 90th minute the nineteen-year-old Portugal star Cristiano Ronaldo realized that his team was going to lose. It was his first major international soccer tournament. When the referee finally blew his whistle to the end of the game, Ronaldo fell to the ground in tears. It was a heartbreaking loss for him and his team.

For Greece, it was their greatest win in team history. There were celebrations throughout Greece and around the world. Banners went up throughout Greece, with the slogan Νενικήκαμεν "We Won." It was a joyous occasion that the *New York Times* described as "The God's Smiling on Greece."

After the tournament, Otto Rehhagel was hailed a national hero. He was called King Otto. I decided to visit Greece that summer to soak in the festivities. When I go there, friends and family would ask me, "Did you see what we did? Wasn't that amazing?" I would tell them that nobody imagined that Greece could do it. But they did!

Why is the Greece's victory so important? And why is it important to teachers? The Greece team was not expected to win or play at the level of the other teams in the tournament. But Greece was a good team and all twelve players on the field wanted to win. While this book is not about soccer, it is about grit and a big heart, something that both the Greece 2004 soccer team and all successful teachers share. Teaching is no doubt difficult, and successful teaching is not just about making it by as a teacher. Making it by typically requires only the bare minimum and not much heart or effort. Success, on the other hand, achieves more than what is expected from someone. Thus, this book is about the teaching profession and what it takes to become a successful teacher.

# Chapter 1

# Defining Success in Teaching

What is success and how is it defined? This is a question many people ask themselves. Are you successful? If so, why? Is it because you make a lot of money? Is it because you can run faster or jump higher than your friends? Or is it because you have received many awards and medals? Ralph Waldo Emerson, the notable American essayist, defined success as follows:

> Success: To laugh often and much, to win the respect of intelligent people and the affection of children, to earn the appreciation of honest critics and endure the betrayal of false friends, to appreciate beauty, to find the best in others, to leave the world a bit better, whether by a healthy child, a garden patch, or a redeemed social condition; to know even one's life has breathed easier because you have lived. This is to have succeeded!

Emerson's definition of success could have just as easily been conceived with teachers in mind. Successful teachers often laugh with their students; they win their students' trust, respect, and affection; and seek to learn from others even from those that criticize them and long for their failure. Good teachers appreciate the beauty of their craft and find good in all their students regardless of who they are while seeking to make the world a better place.

If you asked several people how they would define success, you would probably get many different answers. But unlike most professions, success in teaching is not just about how many students get A's or B's, or how many students graduated and went on to college, but success is about those small milestones teachers make each day to make a difference in their students' lives. But how does one define success in teaching?

Let's take, for example, two teachers. Teacher A teaches in a wealthy community in Palo Alto, California, while Teacher B teaches in an impoverished community in Detroit. Both teachers are charged by their principal to help their students read at or above a fifth-grade level by the end of the school year. Teacher A's fifth-grade students come into her class reading at about a fourth-grade level. By the end of the year, she has her students reading at an advanced fifth-grade level. Teacher B's fifth-grade students from Detroit come in reading at about a first-grade level. By the end of the year, Teacher B's students are at a fourth-grade reading level.

From these two examples, only Teacher A has met her principal's charge, while Teacher B has not. But are both teachers still successful? If so, could we also say that Teacher B is just as successful as Teacher A, even though she has not met her principal's goals? Surely, Teacher B has achieved a considerable level of success by bringing her students three grade levels up in reading, which is more than Teacher A's students. So, we can say that Teacher B is successful and may even be more successful than Teacher A.

Let's say for now both teachers are successful. The question then is, how do we know that both teachers are successful? We could agree that for both teachers to be considered successful, their students need to be successful. Success in this case is determined by how well both teachers did in improving their students' reading—not by how each teacher engaged her students during a lesson, or what the principal and other teachers in the school had to say about her (which could also be used in determining teacher success). But in this case it was by helping her students improve in their reading.

We could also assume from both examples, student reading improved based on their reading test scores. Using standardized tests to measure and evaluate student success and tying it to teacher performance is a valid way in measuring teacher success, but it is not the only way or the best way. We will revisit this later in this book. But first attempt to answer the following eighth-grade graduation questions from Saline County, Kansas, in 1895.

### Grammar (Time: 1 Hour)
1) Give nine rules for the use of Capital Letters.
2) Name the parts of Speech and define those that have no modifications.
3) Define verse, stanza and paragraph.
4) What are the principal parts of a verb? Give principal parts of do, lie, lay, and run.
5) Define case, illustrate each case.
6) What is punctuation? Give rules for principal marks of punctuation.
(7–10) Write a composition of about 150 words and show therein that you understand the practical use of the rules of grammar.

### Arithmetic (Time: 1.25 Hours)
1) Name and define the fundamental rules of arithmetic.

2) A wagon box is 2 feet deep, 10 feet long, and 3 feet wide. How many bushels of wheat will it hold?

3) If a load of wheat weighs 3,942 lbs., what is it worth at 50 cts. Per bu, deducting 1050 lbs. For tare?

4) District No. 33 has a valuation of $35,000. What is the necessary levy to carry on a school seven months at $50 per month, and have $104 for incidentals?

5) Write a bank check, a promissory note, and a receipt.

**U.S. History (Time: 45 Minutes)**

1) Give the epoch into which U.S. history is divided.

2) Give an account of the discovery of America by Columbus.

3) Relate the causes and results of the Revolutionary War.

4) Show the territorial growth of the United States.

5) Who were the following: Morse, Whitney, Fulton, Bell, Lincoln, Penn, and Howe?

6) Name events connected to the following dates: 1607, 1620, 1800, 1849, and 1865.

**Geography (Time: One Hour)**

1) What is climate? Upon what does climate depend?

2) How do you account for extremes in climate?

3) Of what use are rivers? Of what use is the ocean?

4) Describe the mountains of N.A.

5) Name and describe the following: Monrovia, Odessa, Denver, Manitoba, Hecla, Yukon, St. Helena, Juan Fernandez, Aspinwall, and Orinoco.

6) Name and locate the principal trade centers of the U.S.[1]

This was a sample of questions from an eighth-grade exam from Kansas public schools in 1895. There were also questions on health, science, and orthography (spelling). Were you able to answer any of the questions? A few, perhaps? None? No worries. You had no time to study for it. Right?

When I first started teaching high school, these questions were posted on a corkboard in the teachers' workroom at the school I taught. Every so often a teacher would come into the room, read the questions to themselves, and say to whoever was in the room, "Wow, see what kids knew then, now they can't even write a proper sentence." But what do these questions tell us about how kids learned in the late nineteenth century. It was pretty much rote memorization.

How successful you were in school during this time was based on how well you were able to memorize information, not what you did with the information afterward. This was true for most schools around the world at the time. Students learned to memorize and not to analyze information. Analysis is the process in which we come to understand something or determine the essential features of something and its relations, whereas memorization simply means to commit to memory or to remember. Many of us do not have a good memory, and we can easily forget information we learned almost as soon as we memorized it.

That is why in 1956, Benjamin Bloom and several of his collaborators came up with a simple way to help students learn information. It was called *Taxonomy of Educational Objectives*, or simply known today as Bloom's Taxonomy. Bloom's framework for learning is being used by K-12 teachers and college instructors today.[2]

The original framework consisted of six major categories along a continuum that moved from concrete knowledge to more complex or abstract knowledge: Knowledge, Comprehension, Application, Analysis, Synthesis, and Evaluation. Each category contained subcategories, but the idea was that as the student moved up the categories, she would put the information she learned into practice and thus more likely to remember the information.

Since its inception, Bloom's Taxonomy has taken many variations all of which can be applied to specific grade levels or subjects. But the framework and how it is used are pretty much the same. Bloom's framework was a breakthrough in the way we thought about how children learned and how teachers taught their students. It shifted teaching from getting students to memorize information to analyze information.

One could also make the argument that teacher success is determined by student success. Gloria Ladson Billings argues that for a teacher to be successful, her students must experience academic success.[3] Moreover, regardless of social and economic inequities that students may encounter in their

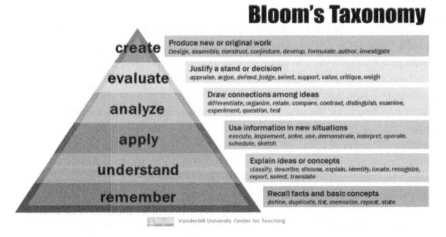

Figure 1.1   Bloom's Taxonomy. *Source:* Courtesy of Vanderbilt University.

lives, all students must be given the tools and resources to achieve academic excellence.

Ladson Billings says, for this to happen it "requires that teachers attend to students' academic needs, not merely making them 'feel good.'"[4] In other words, the occasional positive reinforcement to a student, such as "Great Work!" "That is Awesome!" "You're Great!" is not enough. Teachers of all students, regardless of a student's race, class, gender, or ethnic background, are to challenge their students and help their students grow socially, emotionally, and academically.

Billings's definition moreover gets to the notion of what type of teacher one should seek to be. Should a teacher only seek her students' approval by making them feel good about themselves by regularly giving them simple and unchallenging tasks? Or should a teacher constantly challenge her students even if she risks being disliked by her students? Which teacher has best prepared her students for success? And which teacher will students look back and say Ms. So and So really helped prepare me for college? Which teacher do you plan to be?

This is the challenge that many new teachers face. It is easy to be the nice teacher, the fun teacher, or even the cool teacher, but what does that to do for your students? And will that make you a successful teacher? Billings further argues that there is nothing wrong with "tough-love." It is true that many kids need tough love, they want it, they need it, and while kids say that they don't like rules or someone telling them what to do, kids generally like structure, especially when it comes down to learning in the classroom.

To echo Billings, Geoffrey Canada argues that while school resources are important, they are not the main contributing factor to student success. Rather a child's family background and a child's support network outside of school are the most important factors in student success.[5] yes

Teachers can surely play a big part to help support their students outside of school. This is perhaps most evident in the Frontline documentary *The Education of Omarina*.[6] The film tracks the school life of Omarina Cabrera, a teenage girl from the Bronx in New York City. With her family life in disarray, Omarina's grades drop and she considers dropping out of school. Eventually, Omarina finds support from her teachers and school counselors. She gets into a prestigious private boarding school on a full scholarship, which invariably takes her away from the turmoil of her family and neighborhood. She gets good grades and goes on to college at George Washington University on a scholarship.

While watching the film, it's hard not to think what Omarina's life would be if she did not have her teachers and counselors to support her education. Omarina, however, is not a special case; she is like millions of children around the world who cannot succeed in school because there is nobody who is helping them through the educational process.

A study by Rhodes, Grossman, and Ress found that mentoring is perhaps the most important factor to student success.[7] The authors concluded that "mentors can positively influence adolescents' behaviors, school attendance, and sense of competence in school, so the expansion of high-quality mentoring should continue."[8] The more people behind a student, the more likely that that student will graduate high school and go on to college.

Today, organizations like OneGoal target at-risk teens, help them graduate from high school, and continue to track and support their academic success through college with incredible results. In the West African country of Benin, young girls are assigned a mentor when they begin school. The mentor, who is typically an older girl, helps advise them, walks them to school, works with them on their homework, and even helps them bathe. Benin has found incredible success through this low-cost, yet efficient, mentoring program.

The educational theorist Ken Robinson argues that for someone to succeed they need to experience failure.[9] In this way, and in other ways, one discovers what works and what does not work. What is most important, however, is what one does with that failure. Do they just give up, or do they try to learn from it? Teachers learn from their failures each day. I have never met a good teacher who has said to me that all their lessons were always perfect. And if they did, they weren't being honest. Teaching is an art and not a science. There is no magic formula or silver bullet in teaching. Each day is different, and each set of students each year is different.

My first year of teaching, I taught International Baccalaureate (IB) diploma students. At the beginning of the year, I asked one of the veteran teachers (who happened to be a Jeopardy winner) what advice he had to give me in helping my students score well on their IB history exam at the end of the year. He said, "When I first taught this class all my students scored off the charts on their final exam. I said well, I got my game down, that was easy. The next year I taught the class in the exact same way. That year, my students scored below average."

Each year a teacher gets a fresh crop of students with varied abilities, skill levels, and ways of learning. It is important for a teacher to know her students' strengths and weaknesses if she is to help them succeed. Teachers fail in their lessons: the activities they assign to their students and the way they teach something. This is not unusual and there is nothing wrong with this.

A lesson may work great one year but fail the next. A lesson could even work great during a first-period class but fall apart when it is taught again to fifth-period students. It is what the teacher does afterward matters. Does the teacher do nothing, and say, "Well my students are just not smart enough," or does the teacher try to figure out what went wrong and try to help her students understand the material? The question is, does the teacher care about how the lesson went? Often, after I watch a teacher teach a lesson, they say to me,

"It didn't go as I planned it would go." I tell them, that is going to happen. I then ask them to tell me what they think went wrong and what they would do differently. This is what matters. How a teacher plans to correct her mistakes. Teaching is a process that requires failure, failure that leads to success. I have had students who were doctors and nurses who decided to become teachers. I often ask them, what the biggest difference between teaching and their previous profession was? They tell me that their mistakes can be remedied in teaching, that they do not have to worry about harming their students with the wrong dosage or procedure as they did when they were working with patients. If you give your students the wrong information or you did not teach your lesson as good as you wanted, you could always fix it.

Most people would agree that for a teacher to be successful, the teacher needs to be effective. Charlotte Danielson's *Framework for Teaching* is currently used in many schools around the country. Danielson's framework evaluates teacher performance. Danielson's framework would be less feasible in other professionals such as doctors, lawyers, accountants, or even airline pilots, because teaching is more subjective.

We know, for example, a lawyer is successful because she has won most of her court cases. We know a doctor is successful because most of his patients get well after he treats them, and we know an airline pilot is successful because he lands his plane safely and gets his passengers to where they want to go on time. This is where teaching is more of an art than a science because there is no one way to present material to students, and the way that we teach may vary depending on who we are teaching.

After I watch my students teach a lesson, they usually ask how I thought they did. It's a fair question, but before I let them know, I ask them, how they thought their lesson went? Developing your teaching style, your teaching voice, and even your classroom management style is like fashion. You have to be comfortable with and confident in how and what you are teaching. It has to be who you are. Borrowing from others is great, but making it your own is when you find out who you truly are as a teacher. This takes time but when it happens you know it, because you feel that there is nothing you cannot do as a teacher.

Teaching is also supported by a lot of behind-the-scenes work. This is what is called the "planning stages." Often this takes a lot more work than teaching a lesson. In other words, what does a teacher do before she presents the material to students to assure that her students will learn the material? And how does the teacher know her students learned it? Successful teachers reflect before and after their lesson, which means processing the lesson they taught. Before I planned my lessons, I always considered my students. I was aware of their likes and dislikes and could even anticipate their reactions or questions to parts of my lesson.

A successful teacher should also analyze the results of a test to find where their students may have struggled. If most students did not do well on a question or if there is problem on the exam, this may indicate that some of the material was not covered as effectively as it should have. The teacher then may consider reexploring a segment of the lesson the following day to assure that her students learn the material. If all the students did well on the test, the teacher may think about challenging her students more.

According to Charlotte Danielson, no matter how experienced and skilled a teacher may be, if classroom practice is weak, one cannot be considered a successful teacher.[10] Danielson's framework tries to cover all areas of teaching, with classroom practice being the most significant. Danielson's framework for teaching breaks down teacher success into four domains or categories which are further broken down between five and six subcategories:

1) Planning and Preparation. Divided in six subcategories.
   a. Demonstrating Knowledge of Content and Pedagogy
   b. Demonstrating Knowledge of Student
   c. Setting Instructional Outcomes
   d. Demonstrating Knowledge of Resources
   e. Designing Coherent Instruction
   f. Designing Student Assessments
2) The Classroom Environment
   a. Creating and Environment of Respect and Rapport
   b. Establishing a Culture of Learning
   c. Managing Classroom Procedures
   d. Managing Student Behavior
   e. Organizing Physical Space
3) Instruction
   a. Communicating with Students
   b. Using Questioning and Discussion Techniques
   c. Engaging Student Learning
   d. Using Assessment in Instruction
   e. Demonstrating Flexibility and Responsiveness
4) Professional Responsibilities
   a. Reflecting on Teaching
   b. Maintaining Accurate Records
   c. Communicating with Families
   d. Participating in a Professional Community
   e. Growing and Developing Professionally
   f. Showing Professionalism.[11]

According to Danielson's framework, before a teacher is observed by her supervisor, the teacher would have a pre-observation consultation with the supervisor to discuss the planning stages of her lesson. The supervisor may ask a series of questions to get a sense of how the teacher prepared for her lesson. After the supervisor has observed the lesson, there would be a post-observation meeting between the teacher and supervisor to discuss the strengths and weaknesses of the lesson, and what the teacher could do to improve her lesson.

Danielson's framework is grounded in solid research. Research studies have gone on to show that each component of Danielson's framework is associated with improved student learning. Typically for each domain and its subsections, a teacher receives a score between 1 and 4, 4 being the highest and 1 the lowest. A score of 1 would be unacceptable, 2 developing, 3 proficient, and 4 exceptional. It is unlikely for a teacher with little or no experience to receive a 4 for each domain. Most teachers and teacher pre-service teachers receive between 1 and 3. It is also difficult for even the most experienced teacher to receive a perfect score on each of the domains.

❧ This does not necessarily mean that the teacher is not highly skilled, but rather there may have not been the opportunity for the teacher to showcase her skills in a particular domain. For example, Domain 2D asks how the teacher did in managing student behavior. A teacher may be evaluated on a day where her students were perfect little angels. So, there is really no way of knowing how skilled the teacher is in her classroom management skills. Rather than dinging the teacher for this, the supervisor is asked to only reply "Not Observed."

Currently, most schools and teacher training programs in the United States use Danielson's *Framework* in helping pre-service teachers develop their craft. Danielson's framework is also easy for the teacher to understand and see how she can grow as a teacher. A teacher may be evaluated between four and five times a year by a supervisor or principal.

While Danielson's framework is designed to help teachers, many school administrators are using the evaluation to discipline teachers and even fire them. Danielson warned that her framework should not be used to measure teacher quality but rather to help teachers improve their teaching.

To echo Danielson, Dough Lemov believes that successful teachers should:

1) Set high expectations for students,
2) Ensure academic achievement when planning,
3) Have a structure in delivering lessons,
4) Engage students,

5) Create a strong classroom culture,
6) Set and maintain high behavioral expectations for their students,
7) Build character and trust in their students,
8) Pace their lessons, and
9) Challenge their students to think critically.[12]

According to Lemov, all will help students succeed, which in turn will help the teacher become successful.

Pasi Sahberg, on the other hand, says that success is viewed a bit differently in Finland from the rest of the world. He says that

> Finland is not very inspired of measuring education . . . This is perhaps because [Finland's] definition of success is very different compared to how success is understood in the United States or in much of the world. Successful [teachers in Finland] can help all children learn and fulfill their aspirations, both academic and non-academic. Many educators in Finland think that measuring of what matters in school is difficult, if not impossible. That's why assessment of and in Finnish schools is first and foremost a responsibility of teachers and the principals in schools. They are reporting to parents and authorities how successful their school is in achieving commonly set goals. By this definition, school success is a subjective thing that varies from one school to another.[13]

While the tools we use to determine teacher success may vary from one country to another, we can agree that teacher success is important for student success to happen. The school moreover is also important. We have to remember that the school is not just a physical building, but it is a community of learners made up of teachers, students, administrators, and any other stakeholders who are invested in student success.

In my *Introduction to Teaching* course, which is taken by all my incoming graduate pre-service teacher candidates, I ask my students a very simple question: Are schools better today than they were a hundred years ago? At first, my students are not sure how to answer my question. What my question tries to do is get students to think about education within a historical framework of successes and failures in education over time.

Many people believe that schools have gotten worse. We are constantly bombarded by this in the media and by politicians and policy makers interested in reforming schools. They make comments like, we are falling behind in international tests to China, South Korea, and Finland, or that American children are not learning in school today what they were learning in years past.

Often, we too are at fault for this. We make nostalgic comments about how great schools were when we were growing up. But are schools truly as bad as people make them out to be? Let's take a moment to think about what was happening in American schools, 100 years ago. *Brown v. Board of Education* would not be decided until 1954 and the process of desegregating schools in the South and even in the North would not begin until the 1960s. -

One hundred years ago, in most parts of the world, the exceptional child would find little or no accommodations in school, bilingual and second language instruction pretty much didn't exist, and Title IX was something people would not even consider until the 1970s. In most parts of the world, one only needed a high school degree to teach, corporal punishment was still legal in most countries, technology in schools was chalk and a blackboard, and most teachers still believed that the best way for students to learn was through rote memorization. ●

Much has certainly changed in schools since then. What is more important is how most nations view education today. Most countries see that investing in students could have a long-term positive impact on the entire nation, socially, culturally, politically, and economically. In other words, if our students succeed, everybody succeeds. As cliché as this may sound, most countries spend more on education than they did ever before. Education is in the top five of national expenditures in all twenty of the G20 countries.[14] -

More people today also know not just how to read but what they are reading. Improvements have occurred to educational access and opportunity globally. In 1970, less than 1 percent of women in the United States went to medical school and law school. Today there are more women in American law schools and medical schools than ever before.

Education is also a way out of poverty and while hunger continues in many parts of the world, there are more educational opportunities worldwide than ever before. So, we can say that overall education and schools are better today than they were a hundred years ago. But this does not mean that schools in many communities still do not have the proper resources for students to succeed and that schools are still vehicles for racism and inequality.

## WHY NARCISSISTS AND SOCIOPATHS MAKE BAD TEACHERS

In the summer of 2019, I had the rare opportunity to see Yannis Kalavrianos production of Euripides's *Iphigenia at Aulis*. It was quite a magical experience to see an ancient Greek play performed at the ancient theater of Epidaurus. I was also interested in seeing the play because I had my students read the tragic story. One would expect Euripides's play to be read by classics or ancient history students, but my students were neither: they were aspiring teachers.

When my students read the story, they were uncertain what to make of it. I simply asked them to muse on the question, "why would a narcissist or sociopath make a bad teacher?" But before answering this question, let me go over Euripides's play.

Sometime between the conventional dates of 1260 BC and 1180 BC, a Greek army gathered on the beaches of Aulis about 70 kilometers north of Athens. What brought this army together was not to defend Greece from a foreign invader, but to defend Greece's honor.

A few months earlier, Menelaus, the king of Sparta, did what most honorable Greeks did at the time. He welcomed a guest into his home. This was no ordinary guest though; it was Paris, a prince of Troy. Menelaus slaughtered his finest cow for Paris, gave him shelter in his regal palace, and cared for Paris as if he was his own son.

While Paris was in Menelaus's palace, Menelaus had to leave for a short trip and told Paris he was welcomed to stay as long as he wished and that he hoped to see him when he got back. When Menelaus returned from his trip, he found that all his gold and furnishings were gone, and that his queen had run off to Troy with the handsome young prince. Menelaus was naturally furious.

Paris committed one of the most despicable acts of his time. He took advantage of another's hospitality or *philoxenia*. At the time, when one was welcomed into another's home, the host honored his guest the same way that he would want to be honored if he were staying with his guest. Paris broke this code.

Paris knew well that no Greek would tolerate his actions. But Paris was a prince and he knew that his father Priam, the king of Troy, would have no choice but to defend his son, because defending one's family was the highest honor in all of the Aegean world.

After Menelaus discovered that Paris had abducted his wife, he called on his brother, Agamemnon, king of Mycenae, to help him. Agamemnon, the most powerful king in Greece, had at his disposal one of the largest and most disciplined armies in Greece. He was also always looking for a good fight.

Agamemnon called on his fellow Greeks to gather on the beaches of Aulis where they would set sail for Troy once all the Greeks arrived. While Agamemnon and Menelaus waited at Aulis, they decided one day to pass the time by going for a hunt. The two brothers and a few of their men decided to walk up a mountain above the beach. As they walked up, Agamemnon noticed a stunning stag drinking from a shallow stream.

As the cool wind blew down the mountain and as the sun shined its rays through the trees, the men waited for the deer to pop its head up. Agamemnon carefully placed an arrow on the string of his bow, pulled the arrow back, and shot the deer as it was about to run off. His arrow struck the animal and it quickly fell to the ground. As the men approached the deer, the winds abruptly stopped, the streams ceased to flow, and the birds scattered from the trees.

They all stood staring at the deer. One of the men happened to notice that this was no ordinary deer, but it was the goddess Artemis's prized deer. Everybody in the group froze in place and remained silent. Everybody, but Agamemnon. Agamemnon casually walked up to the deer, dragged it by its antlers, and said, "Screw the goddess and her deer," and he ordered the other men to help him carry the carcass down the mountain.

When the men finally arrived back to the camp, word spread fast regarding what had happened. All knew that there would be a heavy price to pay for killing the goddess' deer. Angry at Agamemnon and the Greeks, Artemis ordered the god Aeolus to cease blowing his winds. Now, the Greeks could never set sail for Troy. Artemis also sent a plague down to the Greek camp, causing many of the men to get sick and die.

Days and weeks passed, and the soldiers became restless. With no winds to sail, the Greeks would have no choice but to go back home. So, Agamemnon had to do something quick. He consulted with his high priest and the priest informed him that the only way to travel safely to Troy was for Agamemnon to sacrifice his daughter Iphigenia to the goddess Artemis.

Agamemnon took the priest's words and sent a messenger to Mycenae to notify his daughter that Achilles, the uber-Greek, wanted to wed her and that she was to report to the camp at once, before he changed his mind.

While the other men at the camp passed the time drinking, gambling, and frolicking with prostitutes, Achilles trained all day by racing battle horses on the beach, which he easily outpaced. He was the ultimate Greek hero: courageous, handsome, and strong. When he is later killed by Paris's poison arrow, all of Greece mourns his death.

But Achilles, like Iphigenia, was unaware of Agamemnon's plot. When Iphigenia finally arrives at Aulis with her mother Clytemnestra, Agamemnon insists that his wife go back and leave Iphigenia. But Clytemnestra, like any good mother, is determined to stay with her daughter and help her prepare for her wedding. As Iphigenia and Clytemnestra wait in their tent for the wedding, they hear a voice coming from outside their tent. Clytemnestra walks outside to see who it is:

**Clytemenstra**
Hail thee, son of the Nereid goddess! I heard your voice from within my tent and thus came out.
**Achilles**
O modesty revered! who can this lady be in front of me, so richly dressed, with beauty's gifts?

**Clytemnestra**

No wonder you don't know me, seeing that you never before set eyes on me;
I praise thy reverent address to modesty.

**Achilles**

Who art thou, and wherefore art thou come to the mustering of the Danai-
thou [Greeks claimed to be descendants of Danai], a woman, to a fenced
camp of men?

**Clytemnestra**

The daughter of Leda I; my name Clytemnestra; and my husband is king
Agamemnon.

**Achilles**

Well and shortly answered on all important points! but it ill befits that I
should stand talking to women.

**Clytemnestra**

Stay; why seek to fly? Give me thy hand, a prelude to a happy marriage.

**Achilles**

What is it thou sayest? I give thee my hand? Were I to lay a finger where I
have no right, I could ne'er meet Agamemnon's eye.

**Clytemnestra**

The best of rights hast thou, seeing it is my child thou wilt wed, O son of the
sea-goddess, whom Nereus begat.

**Achilles**

What wedding dost thou speak of? words fail me, lady; can thy wits have
gone astray and art thou inventing this?

**Clytemnestra**

All men are naturally shy in the presence of new relations, when these remind
them of their wedding.

**Achilles**

Lady, I have never wooed daughter of thine, nor have the sons of Atreus ever
mentioned marriage to me.

**Clytemnestra**

What can it mean? thy turn now to marvel at my words, for thine are passing
strange to me.

**Achilles**

Hazard a guess; that we can both do in this matter; for it may be we are both
correct in our statements.

**Clytemnestra**

What! have I suffered such indignity? The marriage I am courting has no
reality, it seems; I am ashamed of it.

**Achilles**

Someone perhaps has made a mock of thee and me; pay no heed thereto;
make light of it.

**Clytemnestra**

Farewell; I can no longer face thee with unfaltering eyes, after being made a liar and suffering this indignity.

**Achilles**

'Tis "farewell" too I bid thee, lady; and now I go within the tent to seek thy husband.

Euripides's description of Clytemnestra and Achilles meeting is quite comical even for someone reading it today. Eventually, both Clytemnestra and Achilles figure out Agamemnon's sinister plot to kill Iphigenia. They both vow to stop Agamemnon. Achilles even threatens to take his army and leave.

In the end, however, Iphigenia insists she be sacrificed as an act of honor and courage to her father and nation. Before her sacrifice, she gives a patriotic speech which rallies the Greeks to go on and fight. She is sacrificed on a stone altar. Her mother cannot bear to watch her daughter murdered, so she confines herself in her tent where she sobs for days. After Iphigenia is killed, they tell Clytemnestra that as the executioner's sword was about to fall upon her daughter's neck, a deity magically whisked her away and replaced her with a deer.

She knew that this wasn't true, and they only said this to make her feel better. Agamemnon, on the other hand, feels nothing. After his daughter is killed, he orders his men to take down their tents, gather their weapons and belongings, and set sail for Troy. Agamemnon only cares about getting his army to Troy, defeating the Trojans, and getting back home victoriously. Iphigenia suffers a heavy price for her father's ambitions.

Agamemnon is the quintessential narcissist, arrogant, shallow, self-serving, and controlling, but most of all he lacks empathy. Iphigenia, on the other hand, is the typical anguished child of a narcissist she is always longing for her father's love while willing to do anything to receive the smallest bit of affection and recognition from him, only to be perpetually let down. *Me*

Why would a narcissist and sociopath like Agamemnon make a bad teacher? Many believe that narcissists and sociopaths would not be good at anything, but the truth is they can be successful business people, surgeons, and even generals like Agamemnon.

But a narcissist and sociopath could never be successful in teaching. They cannot take criticism well, nor can they put themselves in someone else's shoes. One of the greatest attributes of successful teachers is their keen ability to relate to their students. One cannot effectively teach their students if one does not understand their students.

Most of my students are aspiring teachers. Many have gone on to become successful teachers. On the first day of class, I jokingly warn my students, that if any of them think that they may be a narcissist or sociopath they should reconsider becoming a teacher. Many of them start laughing, but the truth is that it would be very difficult for them to be successful teachers if they were a narcissist or sociopath because of a lack of empathy.

 Empathy is not a weakness, but a strength of social emotional intelligence, which is an advanced human quality. It's a quality that distinguishes humans from most other mammals. No other living species in the world could relate to the degree that humans relate to one another.

Most humans have the ability to feel another's pain, to feel love, to miss someone, to hate, or to be angry. It's humankind's emotional sixth sense, and great teachers have a strong sense of empathy. Teachers often know what a student is going to say before they say it, they know their students' likes and dislikes, they know if their students are happy or sad, and they know how to reach their students.

Empathy is also the ability to be able to reflect, to work well with others, to take blame, to apologize for one's mistake, to welcome criticism and learn from it, to plan, and to work toward making the wrong right. This is what all successful teachers do and while not blatant in his plays, this is what Euripides tells us about teaching.

## A FEW CONSIDERATIONS ON HOW
## STUDENTS LEARN BEST

Traditionally we teach with the assumption that reason should dominate emotion and that the classroom should be a quiet space where students and their teacher objectively engage with facts, figures, theories, and other pertinent information.

But this type of teaching approach contrasts what neuroscientists know about the brain and its functions. Emotion grabs attention and activates normal systems that are key to motivation and that emotional motivation is prioritized in memory.[15] Alice Miller's classic work on children from abused families *The Drama of the Gifted Child* suggests that for a child to grow into a healthy, vibrant adult, the child must have the freedom to express her emotions.[16] In the classroom, the child should be free to speak out and not feel that they do not have the freedom to do so.

Studies show that brain circuits involved in the learning process are the same circuits involved in the emotions of pleasure and reward. Thus, a student who learns a new task, first experiences curiosity, then confusion, then frustration, and finally pleasure once they achieve true understanding or learning. In order for teachers to be successful, they need to be in tune with their students' emotional intelligence. They also need to be aware of how of their students learn best.

Advancements in neuroscience have helped teachers better understand the human brain and its learning functions. But breakthroughs in social and developmental psychology have also assisted teachers in their understanding of how students learn best. Prior to age three, children parallel play. After age three, the child's imagination develops. This is absent in most other mammals. Imagination allows for creativity and higher-order thinking skills. Because a child can't drive a car, she may use an object that looks like a steering wheel and pretend to drive a car. For children ages 3–11, play is imagination in action, whereas for adolescents imagination is play without action.

Jean Piaget (1896–1980) divided the stages of learning for a child into four "Cognitive Stages" or four major developmental and learning stages. In Piaget's first stage, which is the "Sensorimotor Stage" (birth to 2 years), children use their senses and motor skills to learn. In Piaget's second stage, "Ego Stage" (ages 2–7 years), children begin using their imagination to learn. In Piaget's third stage, "Logical Stage" (ages 7–11), children begin to think logically, but with practical aids, and they are no longer egocentric. The final stage is the "Adolescent Stage" (11–16 years on). During this stage, children acquire abstract thought and think logically.

Like Piaget, Lev Vygotsky (1896–1934) was interested in how speech impacted children learning. Vygotsky found that children begin using language as an external tool for social interaction. As early as two years, a child self-talks and thinks out loud. Usually, this happens when the child is by herself. Around the time, the child is in school age (about five years) she can transition and use language to communicate with others. According to Vygotsky, external speech is the process of turning thoughts into words, while inner speech is the conversion of speech into internal thoughts.

Howard Gardner's classic theory of multiple intelligences finds that there are different types of learners: visual-spatial, bodily kinesthetic, musical, logical-mathematical, naturalistic, verbal-linguistic, interpersonal and intrapersonal. One could be more than one type of learner but typically a learner gravitates to one of these areas.

The point is that it is important to know what type of learner our students are if we are to teach them well. But it is also important to understand how our students see the world and to remember that it is their life experiences that help shape how they see the world around them.

In my classes, which are made up mostly of graduate students studying to become teachers, I give my students a simple scenario. I tell them, let's just imagine for a moment you are on the platform in the subway waiting for the train to arrive. Let's say you are going downtown for the day (just to add to their imagination). The train finally arrives, the doors open, and you see that

**Figure 1.2   Howard Gardner's Multiple Intelligences.** *Source:* Courtesy of https://com-mons.wikimedia.org/wiki/File:Multiple-intelligence.jpg Attribution: Sajaganesandip, CC BY-SA 4.0 <https://creativecommons.org/licenses/by-sa/4.0>, via Wikimedia Commons.

the train is filled with people. What are your impressions when the train doors open?

This is where it gets interesting. Of course, a few will say I am looking where I could sit or stand. That is a practical response which is perfectly fine. But some will respond based on how they see the world. For example, one of my students who was studying to be a science teacher said she was worried about germs and the likelihood of getting sick on a train filled with people that may be sick. A soon-to-be language arts teacher was interested in the people in the train and what their lives may be like: "She looks so sad I wonder what happened?" Or "He looks so happy. Maybe he's in love." The history or social studies teacher was interested when the subway was built, what was going on at the time it was built, and if any important people ever took the train he was about to get on. The math and physics people were interested in the speed of the train, how many people it could carry in a day, and how quickly people could travel.

This exercise gets my students to understand that they all learn in different ways, but they also see the world through their experiences. As a student, I was a visual learner; history class was interesting to me because I could easily imagine what I was learning in my head. On the other hand, chemistry was not, because moles seemed too abstract to me and too boring.

But are some students born with a natural interest for certain subjects? Even though chemistry was boring to me, I still admire Mendeleev for developing his well-organized table to help students understand the major elements in chemistry. There are students who are good at chemistry and it comes naturally to them, but are there certain people who cannot learn certain subjects?

It's hard not to notice that as early as three children gravitate toward certain subjects. A parent may have two children that are completely different from one another. One may be more into reading and the arts, while the other may be more into science and math. The ancient Greek philosopher Socrates felt that we were born with knowledge. Many during his time criticized him for this. His critics believed that a baby was a blank slate waiting to be inundated with information, and teachers were to do this as if they were putting "sight into blind eyes." But Socrates understood that some children were naturally gravitated to certain subjects and certain people were born to be artists, scientists, or even philosophers, and it was the job of the teacher to help her students find their talents and then cultivate those talents.

When I first began teaching over twenty years ago in Chicago Public Schools (CPSs), I was perplexed by how my students, who were mostly from Chicago's Cabrini Green neighborhood, were being too social in my class. I took it personal until I learned that the only opportunity they had to socialize with their peers was during school, because their parents were too afraid to let them outside to play in their neighborhood.

Can all students learn? Yes, all students can learn. For many teachers, the question is, do all students want to learn, and are there people supporting their learning? Quite often teachers place much of the burden of learning on their students, but teachers share just as much if not more of this responsibility.

It is true that the good student should seek to question and find answers. How students answer a question should be supported by evidence. Students should therefore be familiar with the literature, theories, and arguments that exist around a topic, but more importantly apply, analyze, and synthesize information into their writing, thinking, and argument.

We live in a world of fake news; alternative facts and that truth doesn't matter. Students can't just make up facts. Facts are facts, and there is truth. A few years ago, I encountered a student that was studying to become an elementary teacher. She expressed to the entire class that she believed that humans and dinosaurs coexisted. When I asked her how she knew this, she said from the Bible. My first reaction was to tell her she was wrong, and she should reconsider being a teacher. But I had to remind myself that as a teacher I couldn't just give up on her just because of what she believed. Scolding a student in front of her peers would only draw her further away from learning. It was my job to continue to provide a safe learning environment where she could learn from the other students even though what she said was not based on scientific fact.

There are some things that a nonnegotiable though, a World War II historian that does not believe that the Holocaust did not occur, or an evolutionary biologist that does not believe in evolution. I would say the same if there for a priest, iman, or rabbi who did not believe in God.

As teachers, we should not forget we are there to help all our students. Yes, we enjoy those essays that our stronger students write, the projects our high-performing students create, and the students that pay attention to us and ask a lot of questions, but the ones that struggle are the ones that need us most. This is something we should not forget.

## A FRAMEWORK FOR EVALUATING
## TEACHER SUCCESS

There is a growing body of literature on effective teaching. Most studies conclude that school resources and other teacher resources and supports are important to achieving teacher success. This book looks at teaching and what one needs to know about the profession. It's not about providing any skills in teaching, but getting one to think like a teacher and understanding what it takes to become a successful teacher.

As noted earlier in this chapter, success may vary depending on who you ask. Typically, what the public expects from teachers is different from what schools, districts, or even parents want from their teachers. These are very different measures of how teacher success is defined.

For example, the public typically sees school and teacher success in broad terms. It expects high attendance from students, good comportment, high scores on standardized exams, high graduation rates, high college admission, and high employment rates after high school. Schools, however, see teacher success from both general and local terms. Questions that may drive success from the local level can be as follows: "Are my students learning?" "How do I know my students are learning?" "Have my goals and objective been met for the day?" "Have my goals and objectives been met for the unit and year?" "Am I managing my classes well?" "Are my students engaged throughout the lesson and is there a culture for learning?" "Do I care about my students?" These are the types of questions one should be asking when determining teacher success.

## NOTES

1. NASA. "Eighth Grade Final Exam from 1895." https://www.grc.nasa.gov/WWW/K-12/p_test/1895_Eightgr_test.htm Retrieved May 11, 2020.

2. Bloom, Benjamin S. et al. (1956). *Taxonomy of Educational Objectives: The Classification of Educational Goals.* Longman, WI: Green and Co Ltd.

3. Ladson Billings, Gloria. (2009). *The Dreamkeepers: Successful Teachers of African American Children.* Jossey-Bass.

4. Ibid., p. 160.

5. Tough, Paul. (2009). *Whatever It Takes: Geoffrey Canada's Quest to Change Harlem and America.* New York: Mariner Books.

6. PBS/Frontine. (2016). *The Education of Omarina.* Retrieved February 15, 2021. https://www.pbs.org/video/frontline-education-omarina/

7. Rhodes, Jean E. et al. (2000). "Agents of Change: Pathways Through Which Mentoring Relationships Influence Adolescents' Academic Adjustment." *Child Development.*

8. Ibid., p. 1669.

9. Robinson, Ken and Aronica Lou. (2014). *Finding your Element. How to Discover your Talents and Passions and Transform Your Life.* London and New York. Penguin books.

10. Danielson, Charlotte. (2007). *Enhancing Professional Practice: A Framework for Teaching.* Alexandria, VA: Association for Supervision & Curriculum Development.

11. Ibid.

12. Lemov, Doug. (2010). *Teach Like a Champion 2.0: 62 Techniques that Put Students to the Path of College.* Jossey-Bass.

13. Sahlberg, Pasi. (2012). "Four Questions about Education in Finland." https://pasisahlberg.com/four-questions-about-education-in-finland/ Retrieved January 15, 2020.

14. Statista. "G20 Statistics and Facts." https://www.statista.com/topics/4037/g20-summit/#dossierKeyfigures Retrieved November 5, 2021.

15. Talmi, Debra. (2013). "Enhanced Emotional Memory: Cognitive and Neural Mechanisms." *Current Directions in Psychological Sciences,* 22(6), pp. 430–436.

16. Miller, Alice. (1996). *The Drama of the Gifted Child: The Search of the True Self.* New York: Basic Books.

## Chapter 2

# On Teaching, Education, and Schools

The story of the teacher is within the cultural and historical fabric of most societies. Teachers play an important role in the lives of children as well as in the community they work in. They pass down social and cultural norms, ways of living and learning, and generally help students learn how to navigate through the world. A teacher's job description often goes beyond just teaching students, and teachers are always expected to do more.

In the wake of the mass school shooting at Marjory Stoneman Douglas High School in Parkland, Florida, in 2018, President Donald Trump proposed arming teachers to help prevent future school shootings. Teachers nationwide were up in arms with the president's proposal. One teacher commented, "Hi, I'm a teacher. I don't want a gun. I could use some more dry erase markers. Thanks for your time."[1] Another teacher said, "I'm a teacher. Don't give me a gun. Give me the supplies I need, the salary I deserve, and the common-sense gun laws to protect my kids."[2] Another veteran teacher angrily commented, "And your solution is to arm teachers? Are you fucking insane? I'm a teacher, I teach children. I've been in the army, I've made the choice to no longer be a soldier, but a teacher!"[3]

While most teachers were opposed to the president's proposal, pro-gun groups and many politicians found the proposal to be a sensible way to help curb the rise of school gun violence. Teachers are expected to do more and many times for less. This chapter looks at what it takes to become a teacher and some of the more recent struggles that teachers face.

## WHO IN THEIR RIGHT MIND!

In the United States, there are nearly 3.6 million teachers in public schools in grades K-12.[4] Teachers are often asked to put more than 60 hours a week in their schools and an additional 10–20 hours per week preparing their lessons at home. In any given workday, a teacher teaches her classes, grades student work, attends meetings, works with students after school, and does it again the next day. At times, teachers feel that they can barely keep their heads above water. One first-year high school teacher, Susan Wei, writes:

> Teaching in a public high school is much more complex than those outside can imagine. Every day, you are running five different classes, designing and adapting learning activities that you hope will meet the needs of your students while simultaneously fulfilling departmental, building, district, and state standards. Most days, you work from 7 A.M. to 9 P.M., often with just a break for dinner. Despite diminishing sleep, you need to maintain an energy level that matches that of teenagers, while remembering to remain the adult in the classroom. And you must constantly remind yourself of the power you have to affect your kids, for better or worse. You can't afford to be careless, indifferent, hurtful, fake, or oblivious (as you might on an off day with adults) because kids never get over it.[5]

Having little or no time to use the restroom, eating lunch while making copies, grading piles of homework, answering emails and phone calls, attending school-wide events, and dealing with student issues is just another day for a teacher. A teacher may interact with well over 100 people in any given day and constantly feel she has no time to herself. Most teachers do not have an office to get some downtime or a proper workspace to grade and plan for their classes. They are constantly on the go from the moment they walk in the door until the moment they leave.

According to the U.S. Department of Education, the average beginning salary for public school teachers in the United States in 2017 was about $59,000.[6] The highest was in California at about $79,000 per year and the lowest was in South Dakota at $42,000 per year.[7] In Chicago Public Schools (CPSs), it was just over $50,000 in 2021. In the United States, 44 percent of teachers are under the age 40 and 56 percent have a master's degree or higher. In 2013, about half of teachers quit their posts in less than five years.[8]

Teaching is not easy, and most teachers do not choose the profession for the financial rewards.[9] According to another study from the University of Chicago, the more challenging a school or district, the higher the teacher turnover.[10] So why would anyone want to be a teacher?

In his best-selling book *Teacher Man*, Frank McCourt reflects on a 30-year teaching career in New York Public Schools. McCourt begins teaching at McKee High School, a vocational school in New York City. After completing a degree in English at New York University and acquiring his teaching credentials, McCourt struggles finding a teaching job. He unwittingly takes a job at the New York City docks, but later decides to give up his career as a dock worker to pursue a PhD at Trinity College in Dublin, Ireland. After a few semesters at Trinity College, he moves back to New York City and gives teaching one more shot.

On his first day at McKee High School, McCourt feels nervous and uncertain what to expect from his students. His students are loud and uncooperative. At one point, a student throws a sandwich on the floor. McCourt calmly walks over and picks the sandwich from the floor and begins to eat it. "EEW! . . . YUK!" are his students' response as soon as they see McCourt eating the sandwich. But this captures their attention.

Later, McCourt's students are curious about him, like his funny-sounding Irish accent, and want to hear more about his poor upbringing in Ireland. McCourt quickly learns that he is not that different from his students. Like them, he grew up poor and struggled to make it through the day. Many of McCourt's students don't finish high school. But McCourt enjoys his students. He cares about them and wants them to learn.

McCourt who is remembered today as a successful teacher and best-selling author was not always a great teacher. It took McCourt several years to master his craft. He was fired from most of his teaching jobs, which he is not ashamed to write about in his books, but learns from his failures.

For most of his teaching career, McCourt teaches in the most underperforming schools in New York City. This is where he feels he learned to become good at teaching. It is only toward the end of his career that he gets a teaching job at the prestigious Stuyvesant High School in New York City. But McCourt loved teaching, and he loved teaching students from all backgrounds. While his teaching career had its ups and downs, the personal rewards that he got from teaching were well worth in the end for him.

Frank McCourt's story is not unusual. His life experience, hard work, and dedication show that teachers are often asked to perform miracles. In many schools, teachers buy their own school supplies, pay for their own photocopies, and even provide their students with important basic supplies, like pencils and paper.

In many developing countries, there are no basic resources, like desks and chalkboards or even a proper floor. While teaching is one of the toughest professional careers, it is also one of the most personally rewarding careers. If you talk to most teachers, they will tell you that the altruistic rewards from teaching are worth it. Given these challenges, nine out of ten teachers in the United States today are satisfied with their jobs.[11] Teaching typically is ranked high on job satisfaction surveys, along with medical doctors, computer engineers, and college professors. Lawyers, police officers, and sales representatives typically have the lowest job satisfaction.

But teachers don't feel like they are always respected, and societal perceptions of them may impact how well students perform in school. Recent studies have found a correlation between the way teachers are perceived in society and how well students do in school. For example, in South Korea and Finland teaching is one of the most-valued and respected careers. Parents even encourage their children to become teachers and even marry a teacher when they get older.

Both nations South Korea and Finland have scored high on international exams like PISA and TIMMS. In nations where students do not score well on these exams, teaching is typically viewed unfavorable. At the same time, to become a teacher in Finland, one needs at least a master's degree, and it is highly competitive to get into a teaching training program. It's hard not to question if we changed the way we viewed teachers in the United States, would this help increase students' test scores in schools? Some believe this would help students better succeed in school.

Teaching is no doubt a profession and a very difficult one. It is one of few professions that most societies see as a decline in job performance with more experience, rather than an improvement as with doctors, lawyers, airline pilots, and nurses. Surely, one needs a high level of energy to teach, and teachers need to be able to relate to their students even when they are so far removed from their students' lives.

Teachers also need to learn new ways of teaching their students, often with the use of new technology and new approaches to teaching. But becoming a teacher today is not as easy as it used to be. In the United States, most states have raised standards on becoming a teacher, and there are fewer and fewer people who are choosing to become a teacher each year.

## ON BECOMING A TEACHER

Today lawyers, doctors, accountants, nurses, and teachers go through a rigorous and regulated process to gain access into their professions. They are expected to achieve a requisite level of education, pass specific examinations, and, for teachers, doctors, and nurses, complete a residency or internship program.

While women were not always welcomed into law and medical schools, teaching has always been a profession dominated by women, especially at the elementary and middle school levels. In the United States alone, nearly 74 percent of all teachers from kindergarten through the end of high school are female.[12] In China, nearly 80 percent of primary school teachers are female, and in Brazil, South Korea, Italy, and Saudi Arabia over 90 percent.[13] From the beginning, women dominated the teaching profession, mostly because women were thought to be natural caregivers but also because they would be paid less than their male counterparts.

In most countries, one seeking to become a teacher in a public school setting is required to have at least a bachelor's degree. In the United States, teachers are required to have a college degree as well as an educator's license or teaching certificate. An educator's license is typically issued by the state (typically by the state's board of education) for which a teacher completed her program.

Requirements for becoming a teacher have recently become more rigorous in the United States, and many teacher-preparation programs have seen significant drops in their enrollments.[14] In Illinois alone, teacher-preparation programs have seen about a 40 percent drop since 2010. After the Covid epidemic, there has been an increase in these programs because of early teacher retirements.

In the United States, states typically decide what one needs to become a teacher. Colleges and schools of education, whose teacher programs have been approved by their state's board of education, provide much of the course work and training.

These programs cover birth to age 21 and are typically organized around early childhood licensure (birth to grade 2); elementary licensure (grades 1–5); middle school licensure (grades 6–8 in various discipline areas); secondary (grades 9–12 in various discipline areas); and music, physical education, visual arts, and foreign language. Some other areas for licensure are special education, library specialist, and gifted and reading specialist. A state also licenses school counselors, teacher leaders, school principals, and district superintendents. In most states, before being admitted into a teacher licensure program, new teachers must pass an entrance exam called the Praxis or Test of Academic Proficiency (TAP), SATs, or ACTs may be accepted in lieu of these tests depending on the state.

Prospective teachers must also demonstrate knowledge in the subject or subjects that they will be teaching. This is evidenced through the course work that a teacher candidate completes at an accredited college or university as well as passing required exams, which tests a teacher candidate's content or subject knowledge.

Once teacher candidates complete all the required course work as well as their practicum/clinical experiences (clinical observations and student teaching), they (in most states) are required to complete and pass the Teacher Performance Assessment or EdTPA portfolio. Once a teacher has completed and passed all these requirements (exams, course work, and clinical and student teaching experiences, EdTPA), the state may grant them an educator's license.

There are also alternative teaching programs like Teach for America (TFA), which allows candidates to receive an expedited teaching license. Teaching candidates in these programs are not typically required to follow the same requirements as those candidates that go through a traditional teaching program at a college or university.

A teacher's license may be suspended or revoked by the state granting body for several reasons. In most states, it is for incompetency or immoral conduct, tax delinquency, failure to make court-ordered payments for child/ family support, or failure to comply with a subpoena or warrant. In 2009, in Illinois, 121 out of 43,670 doctors lost their medical licenses. In 2015, 28 attorneys were disbarred out of 63,211 practicing attorneys, and in 2017, there were nearly 136,000 teachers in Illinois with only 12 teaching licenses revoked.[15]

In the past, teaching was seen as something women could do before they got married and had children of their own. In her best-selling book *The Teacher Wars: A History of America's Most Embattled Profession*, Dana Goldstein found that teachers had to fight long and hard to gain the respect they deserved.[16] But many teachers today still feel that they have not gained the respect that they deserve.

## TYPES OF SCHOOLS

During school days and school hours, one-fifth of the total U.S. population consists of students from K-12. This is an astounding number. In most countries, children are expected to begin school at a specific age and are required to attend school to a certain age. Moreover, most schools around the world are organized around elementary, middle, and secondary schools. In the United States, the school life of the student can start as early as the age two-and-a-half years with pre-school or junior kindergarten and continue on through college and graduate school. In most states, children begin school at age five or six with kindergarten. Elementary school is typically from kindergarten to fifth grade, middle school from sixth to eighth grade, and high school from ninth to twelfth grade. The United States has perhaps the most diverse and unique school types in the world.

### Public Schools

Unlike most countries in the world, where schools are funded by the federal government, state and local governments are primarily responsible for funding public education in the United States. Some monies for schools however do come from the federal government.

Public schools are the most common types of schools in the United States, and most public schools range in grades K-12. Historically, American public schools come out of the Common School movement in the nineteenth century in Boston, when local taxes are collected to help support schools.

Horace Mann, who would later become secretary of education under Thomas Jefferson, was the earliest proponent of Common School and arguably the father of America's public school system . Born in Franklin, Massachusetts, in 196, Mann believed that both boys and girls should be educated because this was the best way to preserve the Republic and Democracy in the United States. He is remembered for saying:

> A house without books is like a room without windows. No man has a right to bring up his children without surrounding them with books, if he has the means to buy them. It is a wrong to his family. He cheats them! Children learn to read by being in the presence of books. The love of knowledge comes with reading and grows upon it.[17]

The first Common Schools were governed by local school committees (school boards). At first, Mann argued that the main purpose of education was to develop the moral character of the child, which was a common mission for most schools in the Western world. Religious instruction was important, and children learned by reading stories from the Bible in what were called hornbooks. Later Mann moved toward more secular education that was open to both boys and girls, immigrant children, and all social classes. Mann also introduced chairs with backs, a school bell, blackboards, and standardized textbooks. At first, many Americans opposed the Common School because they feared large government interference. By the late nineteenth century, however, public schools became common across the United States.

The Common Schools were nonetheless first only open to whites, and schools in the North were segregated between white and black. In the Southern United States, education was not available to African Americans and when it did become available after the Civil War 1861–1865, black children could not attend school with white children and were provided with few resources.

By 1855 schools are desegregated in the North after the *Roberts v. City of Boston* decision. Sarah Roberts, a five-year-old African American girl, was registered to attend Abiel Smith School, an underfunded all-black school. Her father tried to register at a well-funded all-white school down the street from their home but was denied because of Sarah's race. Sarah is also threatened with physical removal when she tries to enter the all-white school with her father.

Sarah's father later filed a complaint to the state legislature. The complaint eventually moved up to the Supreme Court of Massachusetts and the court sided with the Roberts. It is a landmark decision that made Sarah one of the first civil rights activists. The decision led to the desegregation of all public schools in the North.

Today public schools in the United States are primarily funded by local property taxes, with some monies coming from the state and federal government. Public school expenditures rose in the United States from $69 million in 1870 to $149 million in 1890. Enrollments also increased during this period with an increase of immigration to the United States from 7.6 million students in 1870 to 12.7 million in 1880. By 1900, nearly all children attended elementary school and about 80 percent attended high school. Between 1890 and 1930, high school enrollments doubled, and during much of the twentieth century, the United States led the world in universal education. Schools become the greatest symbol of democracy in the United States, because all students, regardless of race, religion, ethnic, or social background, are given a fair chance at education in the American public school.

Today, the largest public school system in the United States is New York City Public Schools with more than 1 million students and over 1,200 schools, followed by Los Angeles Unified Public School system with nearly 700,000 students, and CPSs, with some 400,000 students and 664 schools. China has the largest state-supported school system in the world with nearly 250 million students in grades K-12. According to the Organization for

**Figure 2.1   Black Children Excluded from Attending School in Boston.** *Source:* Anti-Slavery Almanac.

Economic Co-operation and Development (OECD), the United States is tied with Switzerland when it comes to annual spending per student with an average spending of about $11,000 per student.

## Private Schools

Unlike public schools, private schools are privately funded. Much of the funding to operate these types of schools comes from student tuition, student fees, and donations. These schools could range in grades K-12. According to the Council of American Private Education (CAPE), in 2014, there were 5.3 million students enrolled in private schools in the United States in grades K-12. The U.S. Department of Education estimates that there were about 34,000 private schools in the United States. Most of these schools are affiliated with a religious group (e.g., Catholic, Christian, Orthodox, Jewish, Islamic). Catholic schools form the bulk of these schools. Tuition in these schools ranges from $2,500 to over $50,000 per year.

In the United States, the private school movement comes out of reaction to the Common School movement. Wealthy American families typically hired tutors to educate their children, but later wanted their children to attend schools with children of their own social status. By the nineteenth century, however, with the advent of mass immigration to the United States, mostly from Ireland and other majority Catholic countries, the private school movement became mostly a Catholic school movement.

New Catholic immigrants, who settled mostly in cities like New York, Chicago, Milwaukee, Detroit, and St. Louis, raised concern about the public schools and their anti-Catholic and Irish attitudes, as well as a Protestant-centric curriculum in public schools. Thus, many Catholic parents refused to send their children to school.

Bishop John Hughes of New York City led a major protest against the public school curriculum in New York City. Hughes, who would be called "Dagger John" for his persistent and well-articulated arguments, argued that Catholic students were being forced to read from the Protestant King James Bible and learn common Protestant prayers. Hughes and the New York Catholic community were worried that Catholic children would be converted into Protestantism. Moreover, the school textbooks were filled with negative references of Catholics and the Irish with statements like "the Irish are drunken and depraved," and that the Irish were "lazy."

Hughes also argued that the schools were an attack on Catholic constitutional rights. A series of public debates between Hughes (who wanted public monies to go toward private Catholic schools) and those that opposed Hughes's demands took place in New York City. In the end, the courts found that public monies could not be allocated toward private schools because of the separation of church and state, but the public schools had to revamp their curriculum and omit negative references about Catholics and the Irish.

Even though Hughes was unsuccessful in his campaign to use public monies to fund Catholic schools, he helped create one of the most successful private school systems in the world. The Catholic school system ranged from kindergarten all the way through college and university. The Catholic schools eventually gained a reputation of providing a better education than many public schools, and all children regardless of if they were Catholic or not were welcomed to these schools. The schools also were an intricate school feeder system. Students who graduated from a Catholic elementary school typically went on to attend a Catholic high school and then a Catholic college or university.

Other popular private schools are laboratory schools or demonstration schools. Most of these schools are private but some are public schools. These schools are usually affiliated with a college or university and provide training for teacher candidates. One of the first laboratory schools was operated by John Dewey on the campus of the University of Chicago. Focused on experiential learning, or what he called "learning by doing," students at the Laboratory School were asked to build tree houses using the math they learned in their math class, weld steel objects using what they learned in their chemistry class, and gather the types of plants that they read about in their science books. Dewey's approach provided a context for the learning to students and helped answer the question many students often ask, "How am I going to use this later?"

Dewey's education practices were largely built on our understanding of cognitive (brain) research and social research conducted in the twentieth century by biologists, psychologists, and educators. Several researchers made major contributions to the field of cognitive and constructivist psychology during this time and Dewey applied it to his Laboratory School.

Dewey understood that the learning process was complex. As individuals with unique experiences, we construct our own understanding of how new ideas fit into our prior learning. Learners must be actively involved in the learning process for information to be understood, retained, and applied.

Dewey moreover understood that social and technological forces of his time such as industrialization and mass immigration to the United States would all inevitably reshape America's social and cultural fabric. For Dewey, it was important that the curriculum represent and present, with a certain degree of symmetry, all the intrinsic factors in the human experience.[18] In other words, Dewey felt that the curriculum that was in place in most schools did not consider the needs of a diverse America, but instead maintained an outdated outlook of how mostly the white, Anglo-American child learned.

Today, laboratory schools and demonstration schools like John Dewey's are found around the world.

## Charter Schools

According to the educational historian Steven Tozer, "A charter school is one for which the school district grants a group of people, which could include parents, community members, and teachers, a charter or authorization, to open a school that reflects their shared educational philosophy."[19] Charter schools were part of the broader school choice movement that began in the United States in the early 1980s. Mostly an urban phenomenon, charter schools was a desire to provide better schools and better education to children whose neighborhood public schools were failing.

At first, charter schools were welcomed by parents and students, and even the local teachers' unions felt it was a good alternative to the public school system. Later however they were seen as a backdoor to break the teachers' unions, because teachers at the charter schools were not union-ized and unions. To a certain extent this was true. Many public schools in cities like Chicago, New York, and New Orleans after Katrina were turned into charter schools. Teachers who taught at these schools before they were chartered, were fired and had to reapply if for their jobs in the new charter school.

Today, there are about 1.8 million students in charter schools, with about 5,300 students in grades K-12 in twenty-seven states. According to a 2013 study from Stanford University, charter schools educate a higher percentage of students in poverty than all the public schools combined.[20] A much higher number of students in charter schools are Hispanic and African American than in public schools, and a higher percentage of charter school students are English-language learners.

While charter schools began as a grassroots movement for better schools, a better education for children, and more school choice, they became politically contentious. Charter schools were in the beginning predominately operated by the community or teachers but later run by charter school networks that worked much like corporations. Funding for the schools today comes directly from the public school system that derives its money from local taxes. So, CPSs funded a certain amount of money (typically monies that would have gone to the public schools) to a charter school or its charter school network. The organization operating the charter school uses the money to pay for staff salaries, maintenance, and any other operating costs for the school. Whatever monies are left typically go to the charter organization as profit.

Students must apply to get into the charter school because there a certain number of seats are available. But the application is not based on student test scores or performance at their prior school but are admitted by a lottery system. Once a student is admitted, they can feel to be privileged to attend a charter school. But the charter schools have not been performing as some have predicted. In fact, public schools in Chicago perform just as well, if not better than the city's charter schools. Some see charter schools as merely a band aid to a larger problem in education.

## Homeschools

Homeschooling, or schooling in the home, is perhaps the oldest form of schooling in the world. Today about 1.8 million students or 3.4 percent of the school-aged population in the United States is homeschooled. With the advent of industrialization in the nineteenth century, the modern state-funded school was created. Industrialization demanded a robust workforce, and workers needed schools to help support their children and prepare them for the rapidly growing industrial economy. Schooling at home had been primarily the responsibility of private tutors that could only be afforded by wealthy or elite families, but the state-funded school was open to all citizens. As such, we could say that these two types of schools served very different purposes. For much of the seventeenth and nineteenth centuries, homeschools or tutors in the United States were much like those found in Europe prior to industrialization. Individualized lessons between teacher and student. After the creation of the Common School which became the public school, schooling in the home virtually disappeared.

But by the 1970s and 1980s, as the educational historian Milton Gaither points out, homeschooling becomes popular again primarily as a form of protest to public schools.[21] It is first common among white Evangelical Christian families who wanted their children to have a Christian-centered education. Later, it becomes popular among nonreligious and secular groups who feel that they could provide a better education for their children than their local public schools.

Today, we could say homeschooling in the United States has become mainstream and serves students across racial, religious, and socioeconomic lines. Parents of homeschooled children serve as the primary teachers for these children. They are expected to create lesson plans, incorporate standards, and assess their students. In most states, children who are homeschooled are entitled to after-school programs at their local public schools.

The homeschool movement is growing worldwide today and an entire industry is built around the homeschooled student. The movement is expected to continue to grow in the United States and after Covid many parents decided not to send their children back to school but to homeschool them.

## International Schools

The international school movement began at the turn of the twentieth century primarily to serve diplomats and expatriates from Europe and the United States who wanted their children to receive an education similar to the one back home. Since that time, international schools have grown to more than 8,000 schools worldwide, 4.5 million teachers, and more than 420,000 teachers.[22] Almost every country in the world has an international school in grades K-12. Most international schools are private schools and have gained a reputation for providing a rigorous and high-quality education with a global-oriented focus. Important to the curriculum at these schools are the Advanced Placement and/or International Baccalaureate (IB) curriculum. Teachers and administrators at the schools are hired from around the world and students at the school are also from around the world thus creating a global community in the school.

## Virtual Schools

Virtual or online schools allow students to learn outside the traditional "brick-and-mortar" classroom. Virtual schools first began to appear in the early 1990s. Unlike distance learning which has been around in some form or another since the 1800s by using telegram to communicate between learner and instructor, virtual schools allow communication between the learner and instructor via a virtual method or online. Specific platforms, blackboard, canvas, coursecraft, and so on, integrate communications to occur more effectively. Virtual schools have grown significantly since the 1990s. According to Evergreen Education Group, a leading research organization on online education, 523,000 students were served by state virtual schools during the 2015–2016 academic year in grades K-12.[23] Virtual schools are an alternative way to serving students' educational needs, and some students like the model.

## Other Types of Schools

Other types of schools include magnet, schools within schools, and themed schools. Most of these types of schools are found in cities in the United States and are primarily secondary schools. Magnet schools were started in the 1960s to provide a quality education for minority students. It was part of the public school choice movement in many cities. Later magnet schools became hubs of academic talent drawing the most-talented students into the school. They were called selective enrollment because students needed to test to get into these schools. They later however became controversial because many neighborhood schools were converted into magnet schools or new schools were built for high-achieving students. The issue was that city taxpayer dollars went to build schools that were not open to all students. Today Chicago has one of the most competitive admissions into magnet schools. North Side College Preparatory High School, a magnet school, and Walter Payton High School both have an admission rate of about 7 percent, making them more difficult to get into than Harvard University.

Schools within schools emerged in the 1970s mostly in cities. They were developed based on research that students were more likely to succeed in smaller school settings. Large public schools were divided into smaller independent public schools to create a small school feeling within a larger school building. Classes in schools within a school are typically smaller (no more than twenty students) than the regular public school, where student class sizes could reach up to forty students. Today, each of the smaller schools has their own school name, budget, principal, and teachers. Students learn in smaller communities but have access to the resources found in the larger school building.

Themed schools or theme-based academies emerged in the late 1960s. A themed school can be a stand-alone school or one housed within a larger school. Themed schools focus on a particular academic discipline like Performing and Fine Arts, Engineering, Technology, and Business and Finance, or could be career path focused like a STEM. Often these are called career-based academies. Many of these schools require students to complete an internship. In addition to a high school, diploma students may also receive a certificate of study.

## NOTES

1. Anonymous teacher Facebook post February 22, 2018.

2. Ibid.

3. Ibid.

4. U.S. Department of Education. National Center of Education Statistics. https://nces.ed.gov/fastfacts/display.asp?id=28 Retrieved January 18, 2018.

5. Wei, Susan. (2001). "Reflections of a First-Year Teacher: Learning How to Make a Difference Seeing Students Reach Their Potential—or Even Just Try—Can Sometimes Be the Greatest Reward for a Teacher's Efforts." https://www.edutopia.org/reflections-first-year-teacher Retrieved January 16, 2018.

6. U.S. Department of Education. National Center of Education Statistics. https://nces.ed.gov/programs/digest/d17/tables/dt17_211.60.asp Retrieved January 18, 2018.

7. Ibid.

8. Carver-Thomas, Desiree and Darling-Hammond, Linda. (2017). "Teacher Turnover and Why it Matter? What We Can Do About it." *Learning Policy Institute.*

9. Doris Santoro found that demoralization is not the same as burnout. Most teachers go into the profession for moral reasons and when teachers can no longer reap the moral rewards in teaching, they become "demoralized." Both demoralization and burnout lead to teacher turnover.

10. Allensworth, Elaine et al. (2009). "The School Teachers Leave: Teacher Mobility in Chicago Public Schools." *University of Chicago Consortium of School Research.*

11. U.S. Department of Education. National Center of Education Statistics. https://nces.ed.gov/pubs2016/2016131.pdf Retrieved January 18, 2018.

12. National Center for Education Statistics. https://nces.ed.gov/fastfacts/display.asp?id=28 Retrieved January 9, 2017.

13. World Bank. http://www.worldbank.org Retrieved January 9, 2017.

14. See *Illinois State Board of Education* for an example for Illinois licensure requirements. https://www.isbe.net/Pages/Educator-Licensure-Requirements.aspx Retrieved April 18, 2017.

15. See https://www.isbe.net/Pages/Archived-Educator-Quality.aspx?Year=2017

16. Goldstein, Dana, *Teacher Wars.*

17. Mann, Horace. (2010). *Life and Works of Horace MANN. Vol 3.* Nabu Press.

18. Kliebard, Herbert M. (1986). *The Struggle for the American Curriculum: 1893-1958.* Routledge and Kegan Paul, p. 64.

19. Tozer, Steven E. et al. (1998). *School and Society: Historical and Contemporary Perspective.* New York: McGraw-Hill Education, p. 470.

20. Center for Research on Educational Outcomes (CREDO). (2013). *National Charter School Study.* Stanford, CA: Stanford University.

21. Gaither, Milton. (2017). *Homeschool an American History.* New York and London: Palgrave & Macmillan.

22. Wechler, Alan. (2017). "The International School Surge." *The Atlantic.*

23. Evergreen Education Group. (2016). "Keeping Pace With k-12 Online Education." https://files.eric.ed.gov/fulltext/ED576762.pdf Retrieved February 14, 2018.

# Chapter 3

# My Kids

When teachers speak about their students, they often refer to them as "My Kids." If a teacher is referring to her own children, she may call them my "biological kids" or "my real kids." When a teacher says "My Kids," she is really saying that she cares about her students and that she wants them to succeed. But there is so much a teacher can do to help her students and very often teachers pick up where many families and communities cannot.

In Robert D. Putman's *Our Kids*, the author discusses the growing social and economic divide in the United States. In the past, it was expected that children would be better in life than their parents. But for many kids today, the future is bleak. Putman finds that the class divide is much more serious than people thought. Wealthier families have an overwhelming advantage over poor families. Wealthier families have more time to spend together, parents of children from these families could attend their child's school and social events, help them with their homework, and pay for daycare, music classes, tutoring, camp, extracurricular activities, and other enrichment programs. Overall children from more affluent families do better in school, get higher scores on the ACT and SAT exams, are more likely to go to college (and get a scholarship), and have a better chance of getting a good job and living a comfortable life.

Children from poor families are less likely to have a two-parent household, a parent that stays home with them, or even a quiet space to do homework. Many children from poor families work after school, help care for their siblings, and often do not plan to go to college. They are more likely to drop out of school, have children as teens, or be jailed.

For many teachers, this is noticeable. The parents of students from higher-income families typically show up to school events. The parents of children from lower-income families are typically working more than one job just to make ends meet and often cannot attend their child's recital, play, sporting event, or even parent-teacher conference.

It's hard not to see how the system benefits wealthier families. Wealthier families are better educated and better equipped to help their children succeed. They know how to navigate through the educational system. They can afford to live in better communities with better schools. Low-income families are typically afraid to voice their concerns about their child's education. Often, they do not want to be noticed and trust that their child's school and teachers are working toward their best interests.

Today in Chicago, to enter a selective enrollment school, it can begin as early as four or five years old. If the child does well on an entrance exam, she may be admitted into a selective enrollment elementary school. I child could be tested again before middle school/junior high to enter a selective enrollment middle or junior high school, and again before high school. Student test scores and grades determine which magnet school they can attend. For families who are not familiar with the process or parents who do not speak English, it can be a daunting and frustrating process. The increase in college costs each year also makes it difficult for one to see if college is worth it in the end, especially if there is no guarantee of a good-paying job after college.

Like Putman, Steven Levitt and Stephen Dubner in their best-selling book *Freakonomics* found that income levels impact how well children do in school. According to Levitt and Dubner, income levels impact the factors that matter most for student success such as the parents' education level, socioeconomic status, age, language spoken at home, school involvement, and whether there are many books and other resources in the home that support the child's learning.[1] Parents from high-income brackets are also more likely to read to their children, travel and go on vacation with their kids, take their kids to a museum and other cultural sites, and work with their kids on homework.

But these economic divides are not happening just in America's cities. Poverty, lack of proper school resources, and limited opportunities are almost just as common in the heartland. In fact, there are more children in poverty in the United States than in any other nation in the developed world. But as the economic divide grows so does the cultural and political divide. A kid from Chicago has more in common with a kid from San Francisco who lives 2,000 miles away, than a kid 50 miles outside of Chicago. This divide is not blue states and red states, but cities and rural towns. A kid who grows up in a city is more likely to travel outside of North America, speak a second language, visit an art museum, attend a play or musical, and interact with someone who is ethnically, religiously, or racially different from themselves.

The same kid is also less likely to learn how to drive at sixteen years, hunt and fish, play a sport in school, attend religious services, know all his neighbors, or have visited a farm. While rural and urban children may identify as being American, they also see the world in completely different ways. The kid in the city is likely to see himself as part of a global community perhaps as being more cosmopolitan more worldly, while the kid from a rural town may view himself as part of a local or regional community.

These same students may also view history and what it means to be American very differently. Is our past plagued with injustice, greed, and cruelty? Or does it embody heroism, patriotism, and success? Unlike most nations, the United States does not have a standard national curriculum. School districts and states decide what will be taught in schools. Toni Morrison's *Bluest Eye* which is taught in many public high schools in New York City is not taught in most rural high schools in the United States. The issue becomes how do stakeholders decide what to keep or take out from the school curriculum and textbook. Is George Washington Carver more significant than Alexander Gram Bell? Should students read the *House of Mango Street* or *The Catcher and the Rye*? And is the Haymarket Incident just as important as the Battle of the Alamo? Recently, we have seen how passionate parents could be, when school boards meetings erupt into shouting matches over what should be taught in schools.

The treatment of history may also differ by school district and state. Was the nation influenced by early Christian ideals or by the secular ideas of the European Enlightenment? Was the Civil War primarily over state rights or slavery? And was Christopher Columbus an ambitious explorer or an inhumane conqueror? But it is also the symbols that we present to students that differ from one part of the country to the other. For a student from the South, the confederate flag may represent something entirely different from a student who lives in Massachusetts. Figures and events may differ from state to state. Clementine Hunter may be more significant to a New Orleanian than an Oregonian. A Californian may care less about Texas history, a required course in all Texas high schools, than a Texan may care about the Pullman-Man strikes, an important social event that impacted the industrial North. The prominent educational historian Jonathan Zimmerman finds that every nation seems to invent certain parts of its history and to "forget" others, and that in most countries various versions of nationhood often inspire acts of courage and compassion.[2]

The history and the curriculum we teach in schools are no doubt guilty of excluding people, groups, and events. Teachers are able to cover only so much in a school year. We want our students to relate to the curriculum, feel that they are part of something bigger, that they share something in common with others, and learn about people who are like them, who experienced some of the same struggles they do, that way they can relate to the place in which they live and to the events that directly impact their lives. This has come at the expense of keeping them in their comfort zones and not interacting with children whose lives may be different from their own. Their behavior and what they are searching are also being tracked, giving them more of what they want and less of what they don't know about. Many students have created these niche cultural silos, where their beliefs are verified and confirmed, and their sensitivities are comforted. Their teachers have told them that they could do or be whatever they want when they grow up, when the truth is that they can't, especially if they don't work hard to achieve their goals. Yes, teachers are there to encourage and support their students, but it is not the teacher's job to promote a student's dream or give them a false sense of hope, it is their job however to help their students find their talents and to help them cultivate those talents.

Over thirty years ago, Alan Bloom warned in his *Closing of the American Mind* on the mediocrity of education—how teachers were not challenging their students and how the school curriculum was not preparing students for the real world.[3] Bloom's book was controversial and does deserve its share of criticism, especially because it ignored the issue of race in America. However, many teachers today are afraid of making their students uncomfortable, they are afraid of challenging their students' beliefs. They don't give their students the grade they deserve, and often they do not tell them that they are wrong.

Challenging our students may hurt our students' feelings, but the reward of learning in the end is worth it. I tell my aspiring teachers what type of teacher do you want to be, the well-liked teacher who does not challenge her students, or the teacher that challenges her students, but at the same time risks the chance of being disliked by her students? As a high school teacher, I felt I succeeded when my students came back years later and thanked me for challenging them, because they felt they were prepared for college.

While it is difficult not to notice that "My Kids" from inner-city Chicago are not the same kids in Kankakee, Illinois, kids today do share many similarities. They are the most socially accepting generation in history, they are more politically active than past generations, and they are determined to be agents of change. We hear teachers describe students getting more and more apathetic or even lazy that their students are more concerned about video games and posting on social media than doing their homework. The truth is that we have always been concerned about each generation, but, in the end, each generation rises to the occasion when they have to.

Millennials and Centennials are not lazy; they are skillful multitaskers who can balance school, work, and have an active social life. We have loaded them with more homework in school, we expect them to do more after school, we want them to perform well in tests and homework, and we pressure them to go to college while not giving them the time and tools to process what they learn in school. They are constantly on the go and looking for the next big thing. They are worried about paying for college and whether it will be worth it for them.

Gone are the days of the smoke-filled coffee houses and musty-smelling college bars, where my generation sat for hours talking about whether there was a God, why communism failed, or what the world would be like in thirty years. We had time to talk and to think. Most of us did not have to work to pay for college. We were sure that we would have jobs after college and good-paying jobs in what we studied.

For today's generation, there are no guarantees. We have tested and tested kids to the point where they have learned to game the system. We have told them they can do whatever they dream and coddled them from the realities of the life and the world. In her famous TED talk on vulnerability, Brené Brown says:

> And we perfect, most dangerously, our children. Let me tell you what we think about children. They're hardwired for struggle when they get here. And when you hold those perfect little babies in your hand, our job is not to say, "Look at her, she's perfect. My job is just to keep her perfect—make sure she makes the tennis team by fifth grade and Yale by seventh." That's not our job. Our job is to look and say, "You know what? You're imperfect, and you're wired for struggle, but you are worthy of love and belonging." That's our job. Show me a generation of kids raised like that, and we'll end the problems, I think, that we see today.[4]

We no longer reward children for what can't be measured, their imagination, their creativity, and their kindness and concern for others. In Denmark, children are taught the importance of empathy. Preschoolers and grade school students are taught to recognize different emotions, articulate experiences, and connect with each other. Denmark's children are some of the best educated in the world and it is in large part because of this early training in empathy. Encouraging imagination and creativity has only helped nations like the United States succeed. Today we are doing less and less to develop our students' imagination and creativity.

We no longer reward children for what can't be measured, their imagination, their creativity, and their kindness and concern for others. We no longer look for ways to help students overcome their fears and transform those fears into curiosity. This is a true gift because curiosity feeds learning and helps answer life's big questions. In Denmark, children are taught the importance of empathy. Preschoolers and grade school students are taught to recognize different emotions, articulate experiences, and connect with each other. Denmark's children are some of the best educated in the world and it is in large part because of this early training in empathy. Encouraging imagination and creativity has only helped nations like the United States succeed. Today we are doing less and less to develop our students' imagination and creativity.

## FROM FIRE TO ACTIVE SHOOTER DRILLS

Studies show that it is more likely for a high school student to abuse drugs than join a gang. It is also more likely for a mass school shooting to occur in an upper-middle-class white suburban school than a poor inner-city black school. In previous chapters, I mentioned how I ask aspiring teachers if schools are better today than they were in the past. The truth is schools are generally better today but not when it comes to the level of violence that is occurring in schools today.

In the 1980s, there were thirty-nine school shootings in the United States that resulted in the deaths of forty-nine people. The decade of the 1990s witnessed sixty-two school shootings with eighty-eight people killed. In the first decade of the twenty-first century, there were 63 school shootings and 107 people killed. From 2010 to 2018, there have been 149 school shootings with 161 people killed. It is true, however, that most gun violence occurs in cities, usually in neighborhoods.

In Chicago alone, 3,347 people were shot in 2016.[5] In 2017, nearly 3,000 people were shot.[6] Many of those killed were teenagers and young adults. School shootings in other parts of the world are nowhere near the level they are in the United States. In fact, most countries have never had a school shooting. And countries such as Germany and the United Kingdom have enforced strict gun regulations to keep it from happening again. As I write this, more school shootings would have already taken place and more children would have been killed.

Just recently a student of mine told me about a shooting at Dixon High School in Dixon, Illinois, where he teaches. He was in the building just a few feet away from the shooter when it happened. A student came to the school with a handgun, shot at a teacher four times, missed the teacher, was later confronted by an armed police officer in the building, shot at the police officer but missed him, and the officer shot the student on the shoulder.

The student survived and no one was hurt. The police officer was hailed a hero, which no doubt he was. When I asked my student where the high school student got the handgun, he told me his mom bought it for him when he was fourteen years old. When I was teaching high school over twenty years ago, one of my students was shot and killed by his stepfather in his home. It shocked the school community and nothing like this had ever happened before to a child from my school. Today it seems that society has become desensitized when it comes to school shootings or when a child is shot and killed.

Forty years ago, most kids worried about having their lunch money taken away in school. Today, many American students live with the real fear that they could be shot and killed in school. No one seems to agree on what the causes of mass school shootings are. Is it guns? Is it video games? Is it Facebook, Instagram, Twitter, TikTok? Or is it the breakup of the community and the family? For many in the United States, protections under the Second Amendment should not limit one's ability to own a gun as it is clearly stated in the Constitution, "The right of the people to keep and bear Arms, shall not be infringed." For many to challenge this right is to challenge the very principle for which the United States was founded. The amendment does not, however, define "arms." Strict literalists of the U.S. Constitution would say any gun is fine, including high-powered weapons like machine guns, perhaps even a bazooka. Others would say that the forefathers would have never imagined the destructiveness of modern guns and bullets, nor would they advocate for criminals and children to bear any type of arms.

Mass school shootings nonetheless are part of the great gun debate in the United States, and they are a major concern of millions of students. The National Rifle Association (NRA), who is against most gun control regulations, argues that there will always be bad guys who will have guns, and the only way to stop a bad guy with a gun is a good guy with a gun. Those in favor of strict gun control regulation find it hard to believe that there is no correlation between the accessibility of guns and an increase in school shootings. How school buildings were designed will differ from how they are being built today. Architects are incorporating bulletproof walls and windows, safe lock doors, and quick exits for students to get out in case there is a shooter in the building.

Disparaging and often divisive opinions on guns were not as prominent as they are today, nor were they part of the school life of children. In the 1970s, TV sitcom *All in the Family*, the brutally outspoken and equal opportunity hater Archie Bunker offers what he sees to be a sensible solution to quelling airplane hijackings, he says, "Arm all the passengers." Immediately after his comment, loud boisterous laughs break out in the audience. Archie Bunker thinks he is just offering a commonsense solution to a real-world problem. The audience, on the other hand, thinks it's ridiculous. While Archie Bunker's solution in 1972 was seen silly, today some find it as a sensible solution to America's mass shooting problem.

Around the same time that *All in the Family* was being televised, James Ingraham, an eighth-grade student at Charles R. Drew Elementary School in Miami, Florida, was accused by a teacher for not leaving the stage of the school auditorium fast enough after a school play. Ingraham was sent to the principal's office and asked by the principal Mr. Willie J. Wright Jr. to bend over so he would be paddled. Ingraham refused and the assistant principal and the principal's assistant restrained him while he was paddled over twenty times. The paddling was so severe that Ingraham suffered hematoma that needed medical attention. Ingraham's parents sued Mr. Wright Jr. for "cruel and unusual punishment." The case *Ingraham v. Wright*, through appeal, went up to the U.S. Supreme Court. In a 5-4 decision, the Supreme Court upheld that "cruel and unusual punishment" did not apply to the paddling of children in schools and that corporal punishment in school was not in viola-tion of the Eighth and Fourteenth Amendments.

The *Ingraham v. Wright* case was the first legal battle brought to the U.S. Supreme Court that challenged corporal punishment in schools. Today nine-teen states permit corporal punishment in schools. In only two states, corporal punishment is prohibited in private schools. In Mississippi, 223,000 students or 7.7 percent of the state's public school population were physically disci-plined during the 2005–2006 academic year. In Alabama, Georgia, South Carolina, and Louisiana, corporal punishment could be used as a last resort for disciplining the child. For example, the Alexander City School's *Student/ Parent Information Guide and Code of Conduct* states,

> As a last resort to maintain discipline or to enforce school rules prior to expul-sion, a principal or designee may administer corporal punishment through moderate use of physical force or physical contact. Such punishment shall be administered under conditions, which do not hold the student to ridicule or shame and which punishment is never in the presence of other students.[7]

Similarly, the *Student Policies Handbook* for the Bibb County School District in Georgia asserts,

> In order to establish and maintain an educational climate conducive to learning, the Board permits reasonable corporal punishment in the schools of the School System. Corporal punishment shall be defined as any action resulting in discom-fort of a student, for example: paddling or exercise.[8]

Poor, minority children, and children with disabilities are two to five times more likely to undergo corporal punishment in school. When questioned in 2013 on the paddling of a student at the Lowndes School district in Georgia, the school superintendent responded, "The reality is that for teaching and learning to occur there must be order."[9] The superintendent was supported by the school board for his decision to paddle the student. While corporal punishment is rarely administered in most states today where it is still law-ful, since the 1970s more and more states have passed laws making it illegal, and in states where it is still legal. An early list of offenses and the number of lashes for those offenses, which were often administered, are illustrated in figure 3.1 in a school in North Carolina from 1848.

The history of schooling in the United States has always been mired with controversy, injustice, and cruelty. It did not begin with the rise of school shootings and the *Ingraham v. Wright* case in the 1970s, but it has been around since the very first days of schooling.

Slavery had been practiced in the United States for over a century before the American Revolution. People from Africa had been uprooted from their homes, ripped from their communities and culture, and transplanted in a foreign and unwelcoming land, to be under the complete control of their white slave owners. They were not allowed an education, because an education would only help them see the cruel injustice being done to them.

The inhumane institution of slavery would continue for almost another 100 years when it is finally abolished in 1865. The practice of slavery is perhaps the greatest injustice to occur in American history, next to the mistreatment of Native American groups. It would have a lasting impact on the psyche of the American people and influence how schools would educate children. But most significant is its lasting impact on the African American community. The black family was decimated during slavery. Families were torn apart,

Table 3.1    **Rules of the Stokes County School.** *Source.* Wm. A. Chaffin Master. November 10, 1848.

| Offense | Lashes |
| --- | --- |
| 1. Boys and Girls Playing Together | 4 |
| 2. Quarreling | 4 |
| 3. Fighting | 5 |
| 4. Gambling or Betting at School | 4 |
| 5. Playing at Cards at School | 10 |
| 6. Telling Lies | 7 |
| 7. Nick Naming Each Other | 4 |
| 8. Swearing at School | 8 |
| 9. Blackguarding Each Other | 6 |
| 10. For Misbehaving to Girls | 10 |
| 11. For Leaving School Without Leave of the Teacher | 4 |
| 12. For Drinking Spiritous Liquors at School | 8 |
| 13. Making Swings & Swinging on Them | 7 |
| 14. For Misbehaving When a Stranger is in the House | 6 |
| 15. For Wearing Long Finger Nails | 2 |
| 16. For not Making a Bow When a Stranger Comes in | 3 |
| 17. Misbehaving to Persons on the Road | 4 |
| 18. For not Making a Bow When You Meet a Person | 4 |
| 19. For Blotting Your Copy Book | 2 |
| 20. For Every Word You Miss in Your Lesson without Excuse | 1[10] |

mothers were separated from their children, children were separated from their parents, and fathers from their families.

Even after slavery ended, institutional racism through the *Jim Crow Laws* continued to further agonize the African American community. "Separate but Equal" in schools and everyday life meant that black and white children in the South could not attend the same school, eat at the same diner table, or drink from the same water fountain. The intention however was to keep black children from going to school with white children. White schools received most school resources, such as the newest textbooks, best-trained teachers, and best school facilities. It took almost another century to end *Jim Crow* with the *Brown v. Board of Education* decision in 1954. The case which ended school segregation continued however to be ignored in most of the segregated South.

After the *Civil Rights Act* in 1964, President Lyndon B. Johnson tied federal funding to public schools which forced schools to change their racist policies. The *Civil Rights Act* further provided 4 billion dollars of aid to poor students, and by 1972, 91 percent of students attended integrated schools in the South. Today the *Civil Rights Act* and the desegregation of schools is seen by presidential historians as Johnson's greatest accomplishment.

But racism did not end in the United States with the *Civil Rights Act*. African American students do not perform as well as their white and Hispanic counterparts today. They are also more likely to be suspended and be imprisoned. But some have argued that racism no longer exists in the United States. After Barack Obama was elected president of the United States in 2008, William Bennet who was secretary of education during the Reagan administration commented:

> Well, I'll tell you one thing it means, as a former Secretary of Education: You don't take any excuses anymore from anybody who says, "The deck is stacked, I can't do anything, there's so much in-built this and that." There are always problems in a big society. But we have just—if this turns out to be the case, President Obama—we have just achieved an incredible milestone. For which the rest of the world needs to have more respect for the United States than it sometimes does.[11]

Bennet believed that Obama's presidential victory, as the first African American president, just proved that there was no longer racism and discrimination against the African American community. After Obama's victory, a fictional tale, known as the "Birther Movement" that President Obama was born in Kenya and not the United States (which would preclude him from being president), was propagated by his political rivals and by New York businessman Donald Trump who said he had conclusive evidence that Obama was born in Kenya and not the United States. Attacks on Barack

Obama's presidential legitimacy left the African American community feeling that their achievement, personal struggles, and perseverance throughout American history had been reduced to mere insignificance. In his wickedly poet prose, the African American writer Ta-Nehisi Coats writes:

> Americans believe in the reality of "race" as defined, indubitable feature of the world. Racism-the need to ascribe bone-deep features to people and then humiliate, reduce, and destroy them-inevitably follows from this inalterable condition. I this way, racism is rendered as the innocent daughter of Mother Nature, and one is left to deplore the Middle Passage or Trail of Tears the way one deplores an earthquake, a tornado, or any other phenomenon that can be cast as beyond the handiwork of men. But race is the child of racism, not the father.[12]

It is difficult for me to personally understand how someone like myself, considered to be a white American, but whose parents just recently emigrated to the United States, is treated better than most African Americans whose families have been here for more than twenty generations. To say that there is no such thing as systematic racism in America, or that white Americans have suffered just as much as African Americans is absurd.

In 1997, Beverly Tatum published her famous book *Why Are All the Black Kids Sitting Together in the Cafeteria.* The book was assigned in one of my courses when I was studying to be a teacher at Northwestern University in the late 1990s. Tatum's book was recently released in 2017 and not much has changed in America since I first read it.

Tatum focuses especially on the many ways in which public policy has continued to hurt people of color most. She points out that in 2008, the housing crisis put the greatest economic hardship on people of color. Tatum also maligns the "gutting" of the Voting Rights Act in 2013, which now allows districts to change elections practices without first seeking district approval. Tatum also focuses on millennials, a group that she calls "color-silent" generation. Millennials self-reported a high level of egalitarianism and a low level of racial discrimination (only 10–15 percent) admitted to personal prejudice against African Americans. Ninety-four percent, however, observed someone treating someone else differently because of their race or ethnicity.

Most saddening is the murder of young black men by the police. After the murder of Trayvon Martin, many Americans put the event within the context of their own lives and own children. What if that was my son, walking home, minding his own business, and he was approached by a stranger. Who is this stranger my child would wonder? My dad told me to be careful if a stranger approaches you in the middle of the night. Yeah, most of them are harmless, but you never know. What if my child did what I told him, what most parents would tell their children, just keep walking, ignore them?

But what if this stranger grabbed my child and my child tried to break his hold and a scuffle broke out between my child and this stranger, a grown man? What if my child was kicking the crap out of this stranger, because my child was scared, because this stranger had harassed and assaulted my child when he was minding his own business? What if this stranger pulled a gun and then shot my child, killing my child? And what if a court found this stranger innocent? Would I not be outraged? Should not others be outraged like me? You expect most Americans to be appalled at what happened to a fourteen-year-old boy, but they were not, because he was black. When the video of the killing of Laquan McDonald by Chicago police was released, one person commented to me in private, "He would have ended up being a criminal anyway, what difference does it make." Dehumanizing people makes it easier to hurt them. The Nazis did this against the Jews and other groups, as did the Ottoman Turks against the Armenian people. The United States is not immune to this when dehumanizing African Americans and other minority groups.

Knowing one's students, understanding their culture and lives is important if one is to help them succeed. African American students are often seen by their white teachers as incorrigible and lacking focus. Christopher Emdin says,

> Too often, when these students speak or interact in the classroom in ways that teachers are uncomfortable with, they are categorized as troubled students, or diagnosed with disorders like ADD (Attention Deficit Disorder) and ODD (Oppositional Defiant Disorder).[13]

A study from Walter Gilliam's further found that as early as preschool, teachers are more likely to discipline black students, because of their own implicit biases and that black students tend to be suspended or expelled at a much higher rate than white students.[14]

One time when I was helping one of my students who was African American at his desk, and I got just a bit too close to him he yelled out to me, "Get out of my face man." Like most teachers, I found the comment inappropriate, and it just may have been inappropriate in all cultural contexts, but to the student, it simply meant you are standing too close to me. As a teacher, I felt it was important for me to point out to my students where we use certain types of language and how we speak to one another. I would tell them, we do not speak the same way to grandma as we do to our friends, nor do we use the same language in church, mosque, or in school as we do on the playground.

Many students don't know that the language they are using may be offensive or rude, they are just using the language they know. In all cultures, language has evolved. Shakespeare often made-up words and today we use many of Shakespeare's words in the English language. In Iran, many young people have given certain words new meanings (often in the pejorative) to avoid being persecuted by the Moral Police that clandestinely roams the streets of Tehran to catch mischievous teenagers. Words and language may mean something different depending on culture; it should not make the language less, but it is important for teachers to be aware of the use of language in cultural contexts, or how our students do not understand in which contexts to use a language.

One year, during mid-semester, one of the school counselors came to my classroom door with a student. The student, who was thirteen years old and African American, wore a finely pressed shirt, black dress pants, new dress shoes, and a new backpack to match his well-coordinated wardrobe. It was as if he was starting his first day of school. I assumed that the student was transferring in from another school and casually asked him what school he was coming from. He said to me, "I ain't coming from any school, I'm coming from jail!" The rest of the class who quietly listened to our conversation proceeded to giggle. I then asked the student why he was in jail for. He said, "Attempted Murder!" I immediately asked him what happened. He told me that a burglar had broken into his family's apartment when he was home alone, and that the burglar tried to accost him, but he ran, grabbed his father's gun, and shot the intruder in the stomach. I was so shocked from the story that without thinking I asked the student if he killed him. He quickly looked up at me and said, "I told you man, it was attempted murder." Boy, did he make me feel dumb! But this was the reality of his world and not mine.

I always tell my pre-service teachers that if you can't think of one good thing to say about a community, you shouldn't be teaching the children of that community. Students I worked with from the African American community in Chicago were one of the most loyal, encouraging, and outgoing students I have ever met. When Travis got up one day to do his presentation in front of the class and froze because he was nervous, the entire class got up and said, "You go Travis, you can do it!" When my class did well on an assignment and I rewarded them with a pizza party, they all ran up and hugged me. When I had broken up with my girlfriend and my students saw that I was upset, they all reassured me everything would be okay because I was a good teacher. When I was teaching about China and naively asked the class when I was not facing them, if anybody had ever been to China, I was welcomed with all their hands up in the air and big smiles on their faces, as soon as I turned and saw them. These were some of the moments of teaching I still remember, when you remember your students.

Many of my students had to grow up fast. They saw things that most people would never see in their lives. Many of them were already hardened when they came to my class, believing they had no future and preparing for the worst. While they lived in communities where most people ended up dead or in jail, I still tried to see them as future artist, athletes, scholars, teachers, and doctors. The odds had always been stacked against them and the community which they came from had always had to fight for success, much harder than most groups.

In the previous chapter, we saw how success was measured in many ways, and there is no one way of defining success. Booker T. Washington, the prominent African American educator and author once, said that success is "measured not so much by the position that one has reached in life as by the obstacles which he has overcome while trying to succeed."[15] This is what the African American community has had to overcome to achieve success.


## WHO IS LIKELY TO FIND KING FAUD'S GOLD COINS?

I tell a story to my pre-service teacher candidates about when I was teaching at the American University in Cairo (AUC) and how I was invited by a friend to join him at Khan Al Kalili market. Khan Al Kalili market or Souk as the locals call it is one of the oldest markets in the Middle East. I was excited when my friend asked me to go with him, because I had not been there and my friend knew how to navigate through the narrow streets of the old part of Cairo.

When we finally got to the market, I was struck by the medieval Islamic architecture that surrounded the hustle and bustle of the market. It felt as if I traveled back in time when the Ottomans ruled Egypt. We passed several souvenir shops, a shisha (hookah) shop, and a café where there were several men drinking tea and smoking. I followed my friend down a narrow corridor that could barely fit a person and as I squeezed through the narrow pass I wondered where my friend was taking me. When we came out from the narrow pass, I was relieved to discover a charming little courtyard masked away from the chaos of the market.

A jewelry shop stood directly in front of us. We walked in and we were instantly greeted by a man from the shop with *Salam*. My friend and I both graciously replied, *Salam* and then my friend asked for Osama. The man stood up and called Osama's name up a winding staircase. A few minutes later I could hear the faint footsteps of someone upstairs. A man came down the stairs, he greeted my friend, reached out, and shook my hand and said, "I am Osama. Welcome."

Osama walked behind a large wooden desk and my friend and I sat at two chairs opposite him as if they were meant for us. As soon as we sat down, my friend asked Osama if he had any new gold coins. Osama looked down on his lap and opened the drawer that was near his stomach. From the drawer, he pulled out a clear plastic sandwich bag. I could see that it was filled with gold coins. He slowly opened the bag and poured the coins on his desk.

The coins were all glowing as if they had just been polished. There were all sorts of gold coins of all shapes, sizes, and each have a different design or logo on it. I starred at the coins wondering where they came from. Then I began to worry. Was my friend doing something illegal with Osama? Was he buying illegal coins? Was I going to end up in an Egyptian prison? Osama saw that I was worried and told me that most of the coins were commemorative from the nineteenth century and that all the jewelers at the Souk sold these types of coins and it was not unusual.

Osama then handed me some coins. I could see one was a British sovereign with Saint George slaying a dragon. There was an Egyptian coin from the time of Muhamad Ali, and there was even a coin all the way from British India. I was curious to see more so I casually asked Osama if he had any ancient coins. He said, "You mean Greek or Roman?" I said, "Yes!" He opened another drawer in his desk and pulled two small Roman coins and gently placed them in the palm of my hand. I had seen Roman coins before in museums but never held one in my hand. I put the coins up to my eye. I could see someone on the coin but was not sure who it was. But I felt like I was holding a piece of ancient history and wondered to myself who else held this coin.

I then noticed that the ridges on the coins were uneven as if someone cut them off. My friend saw the puzzled look on my face and explained how the coin had been shaved and that it was common in ancient times. In other words, if someone shaved enough gold from several coins, they would have enough gold for another coin. "Ancient counterfeitism." My friend said to me. Then Osama started to tell a story.

He said, "Faud I (1868–1936) who would become king in Egypt had four rare commemorative gold coins made when he was a prince. After the four coins were made, they were taken to him so he could give his final blessing for more coins to be made. But before he was able to give his approval, he became king and ordered that the new coins show him as king." Osama said nobody knows what happened to the four gold coins when he was prince, but that they were extremely rare. I asked Osama how much they were worth and he said, "Tens of millions, if not more." But then Osama said, "Is someone from here found it they wouldn't know their value. They would only know the value of the gold their made and not the value the coin. If you know what I mean."

Before we left, I asked Osama how long he was a jeweler. He looked at me and leaned back in his chair. He then extended his left arm with his palm facing the ground to let me how tall he was when he first started working as a jeweler. I then said to him, "And you never came across Faud's coins?" He looked at me and said, "No. But maybe one day."

After we left, I wondered who was more likely to find Faud's gold coins? Would it be a farmer, merchant, teacher, doctor, or someone like Osama in a nondescript jewelry shop in the narrow-winding streets of old Cairo? What someone's parents do for a living, where someone is born, and what someone does for a living sometimes puts them at an advantage. Osama is more likely than most people in the world to come across one of the Faud's coins. What he does for a living and what he knows about the value of certain coins puts him at advantage over most people. Our students may not have some of the advantages that others have because of who they are and where they live.

## PORNOGRAPHY, SOCIAL MEDIA, AND DIGITAL GAMING

Student withdrawal from ordinary interactions seems to be a common trope expressed by many parents and teachers today. Is social media the new drug for kids? Are video games making kids more violent? And are unregulated pornographic and violent websites impacting the way that kids interact with one another? It's hard not to notice teenagers constantly on their phones texting or on social media. While it looks purely innocent and safe, it is not clear what impact social media, the Internet, and video games have on the brain. All these new ways that kids are engaging worry many teachers, parents, and brain development experts.

In the case of social media, behavioral psychologists would say that one only needs to look back to Ivan Pavlov's experiment to understand how social media conditions kids to use it. This is what makes social media so troubling, an unconscious response set off with a prompt. Neuroscientists have found that the *likes* one gets on social media works to elevate dopamine levels in the brain. The more people that like someone's post, the more that person feels good about themselves. But rather than forming a genuine connection with another person, it often makes one feel lonely and even depressed. An unassuming photo on the beach with friends posted on someone's Facebook wall may translate to someone viewing the post as "Oh look at me I am having a great time with friends! I bet you wish you were me?" A former Facebook executive warned users that "You don't realize it, but you are being programmed."[16]

In Susan Greenfield's eye-opening book *Mind Change: How Digital Technologies Are Leaving Their Mark on Our Brains*, Greenfield says that social networking sites could worsen communication skills and reduce interpersonal empathy; personal identities might be constructed externally and refined to perfection with the approbation of an audience as priority, an approach more suggestive of performance art than of robust personal growth; obsessive gaming could lead to greater recklessness, a shorter attention span, and an increasingly aggressive disposition; heavy reliance on search engines and a preference for [Web] surfing rather than researching could result in agile mental processing at the expense of deep knowledge and understanding.[17]

A recent study from Loyola University Chicago found that repeatedly playing video games could lower one's ability to feel empathy.[18]

In the past, parents worried too much about television, but anything that becomes obsessive is bad. The ancient Greek philosopher Aristotle warned about obsessive behavior. He said "Παν μέτρων άριστον" or "everything in moderation." But the social media industry does not want moderation, it wants more and more interaction on social media, more clicks, and more likes because this drives advertisers, and the more advertisements, the more money for the social media company.

Some argue that the way that social media works to get its users is not that different from what cigarette and tobacco companies have been doing years ago. Nicotine of course is the addictive substance that keeps one smoking cigarettes. It is highly addictive, and smokers crave for nicotine. One could ask any former smoker and they will tell you how difficult it is to quit smoking. But it is not just the nicotine that keeps people smoking, but everything that goes along with smoking. The cup of coffee in the morning with a cigarette, a cigarette after a meal, or a cigarette in the car during the morning commute. Like Pavlov and his bell, which conditioned his dog's brain to associate the bell's ring with food, the brain of smokers is conditioned to light up with certain cues. Social media works the same way. The red notification that one gets on their phone sends the signal to the brain that it is time to go on Facebook, Twitter, TikTok, or Instagram account. Once you are there, however, you don't just check out the notification, but you go through your page, see what other people are up to, and before you know it you have been on there for hours.

But it is not just social media that parents and teachers are concerned about, but the easy access kids have to pornographic and violent sites. Like social media, pornography impacts the brain. But this is more profound on children and adolescents, than adults, because unlike adults their brains are still growing and developing. Gary Wilson notes that

primitive circuits in the brain govern emotions, drives impulses, and subconscious decision making. They do their jobs so efficiently that evolution hasn't seen the need to change them much since before humans were human. The desire and the motivation to pursue sex arises from a neurochemical called dopamine. Dopamine amps up the centerpiece of a primitive part of the brain known as the reward circuitry. It's where you experience cravings and pleasure *and* where you get addicted. . . . Although dopamine is sometimes referred to as the "pleasure molecule," it is actually about seeking and searching for pleasure, *not* pleasure itself. It's your motivation and drive to pursue potential pleasure or long-term goals.[19]

As dopamine levels surge, the brain seeks more novelty. It wants less of the same and looks to see new things to get that high. For children and adolescents, this later impacts intimate relationships they will have as adults but use of these sites becomes obsessive behavior for many children. Essentially, there is little regulation on the Internet for these sites. Kids just click that they are eighteen or over and are automatically given access to these sites. So, a kid could see the gruesome beheading of an ISIS prisoner, or the latest Jena Haze gangbang on their smartphone, computer, tablet, or other electronic devices.

Porn sites are on Alexa's top 100 rankings of websites, and YouTube which is a top ten used websites worldwide includes a lot of grisly videos. Everything is out there on the Internet for everyone to read and see. There is little or no regulation. I warn my teacher candidates to rethink using Facebook, Twitter, and any other social media platforms. One principal once told me that she found one of her teachers on Facebook on a beach in Cancun after she had called in sick for a few days.

We have left the responsibility of regulating what children see and watch to parents. But adolescents are far savvier than their parents when it comes to the Internet and social media. They could almost circumvent a block on any site and hide and erase any evidence that they were there. There are a lot of smart people in Silicon Valley, who know how to get people to use their products. They know more about this than the politicians who oversee passing regulations.

The effect of digital gaming may be just as serious on the child's brain. It is hard to believe that children are not becoming desensitized and more violent after playing violent video games. The American Psychological Association finds that violent video game exposure may be related to increased aggression among players.[20] Using two physiological indicators of the fight-or-flight response and on accessibility of aggressive thoughts in children, Douglas A Gentile, Patrick K. Bender, and Craig A. Anderson had a group of their studies participants play a violent game and another a nonviolent game. They then had both groups complete a task after playing the games. The researchers found in the participants of the violent games increased cortisol and (for boys) cardiovascular arousal (relative to baseline) more than did the equally exciting nonviolent game. The violent game also increased the accessibility of aggressive thoughts. The cortisol findings in particular suggest that playing a violent video game may activate the sympathetic nervous system and elicit a fight-or-flight type response in children.[21]

While neuroscientists are still studying the cause and effects of violent video games, current research is finding that these games impact the brain and the behavior of children.

But children are also living in a new age. Industrialization changed the way people lived in the nineteenth century, and the computer and information age is changing the way kids live today. Children today are living in a world far different from their parents and grandparents did. How they interact in the future could be not that different from the way they interact today.

## BUELLER . . . BUELLER . . . BUELLER . . .

John Hugh's 1986 film *Ferris Bueller's Day Off* is about a quick-witted high school student named Ferris Bueller who fakes being sick to stay home from school. *Ferris Bueller's Day Off* takes a humorous look at the life of a well-to-do adolescent from the Chicago suburbs in the 1980s.

During one scene, Bueller's history teacher, played by economist Ben Stein, is taking attendance at the beginning of his class. When he gets to Ferris Bueller's last name, he says in a monotone voice, "Bueller . . . Bueller . . . Bueller" and finally marks Ferris Bueller as absent on the attendance form. For many teenagers, this was a perfect illustration of the rigmarole of high school. Most of Hugh's movies poked fun growing up in the North Shore Chicago suburbs.

In another scene in the movie, however, we get a glimpse of some of the issues that plague kids from families that seem to have it all. Bueller convinces his best friend Cameron Frye to take his dad's beloved Ferrari for a ride to downtown Chicago. Frye is hesitant at first because his father loves his prized Ferrari so much that he checks the mileage to make sure his son has taken it for a drive. Bueller however assures his friend that he could reverse the car's miles once they get back home.

So, Bueller, Frye, and Sloan Peterson (Bueller's girlfriend) begin their journey in a classic red Ferrari while playing hooky from school. While downtown they have a great time, and Bueller even gets to sing on a float during the annual Von Steuben Day Parade. When they get back to Frye's house, they raise the car on a tire jack, put it in reverse, and place a stone block on the gas pedal while they wait for the miles to reverse back. They find out however that the miles on the car are not turning back. Bueller offers to open the odometer and change the miles manually, but Frye insists not to and angrily kicks the front of the car. He breaks the fender and headlights and says, "I'm sick of his shit . . . Who do you love? You love a car . . . I'm just tired of being afraid." He stops for a moment then leans his foot on the car. This causes the car jack to slide off and the car drives off backward into a ravine behind his house. Frye's dad's Ferrari is wrecked.

It is obvious that Frye is struggling at home and what he needs is some attention and even affection from his father who seems to be absent in his life. Suicide rates among children have increased in recent years. The suicide rate for adolescent girls has doubled since 2007. Suicide is the second leading cause of death for children and young adults ages 10–24. Samantha Kuberski is the youngest child to have ever committed suicide in the United States at age six.

White Americans and Native Americans are more likely to commit suicide than any other group, LGBTQ children are the most likely to commit suicide. Adolescents are more likely to commit suicide than adults, and while it is easy to say that kids are just more sensitive today, we need to acknowledge that depression is a real disease that affects millions of children each day.

Researchers have found that children who are cyberbullied and traditionally bullied are more likely to consider suicide. A 2010 study by Sameer Hinduja and Justin W. Patchin found that

> youth who experienced traditional bullying or cyberbullying, as either an offender or a victim, had more suicidal thoughts and were more likely to attempt suicide than those who had not experienced such forms of peer aggression. Also, victimization was more strongly related to suicidal thoughts and behaviors than offending. The findings provide further evidence that adolescent peer aggression must be taken seriously both at school and at home, and suggest that a suicide prevention and intervention component is essential within comprehensive bullying response programs implemented in schools.[22]

Today many teachers and parents believe cyberbullying occurs more often than traditional bullying. Many say this is because of the way that kids communicate today, but the truth is, it is much easier to bully someone remotely than face-to-face.

Stanley Milgram's 1961 controversial experiment showed this when he tested human subjects to learn more about the relationship between authority and obedience. The experiment was set up to demonstrate if people would take orders from an authority even if those orders hurt another person. Milgram's experiment concluded that an overwhelming number of his participants followed orders when given those orders by someone they perceived to be an authority. But there is another dimension to Milgram's experiment: it is easier to hurt someone from a distance, than if that person is nearby.

Milgram's participants were from all backgrounds. They were told that his experiment was seeking to learn what impact punishment had on learning. Milgram divided his participants into two categories: (1) teacher and (2) leaner. The teachers however were being deceived, and the learners were in Milgram's experiment. The teacher was placed in one room, given a list of questions. They would ask the learner a series of questions for which they would hear the learner from a speaker on the wall, and if the learner got the question wrong, they would click a button on a machine for which an electric shock was sent to the learner in the other room.

But to add to the experiment, Milgram had the teacher increase the voltage each time the learner got the answer wrong. The machine listed a danger point "Danger: Severe Shock" and past that "XXX" indicated to the teacher that the electric shock waves were so extreme that they could kill the learner. Once the voltage was increased to a certain point, the learner would refuse to answer any more questions and that they were done with the experiment. The teacher however would be told by Milgram to continue to ask the questions and shock the learner if they got the question wrong. If the teacher was still hesitant to continue, Milgram in a white lab coat would tell the teacher, "The experiment *requires* that you continue." Most of the teacher participants continued to shock the learner. Finally, at 330 volts, the learner would be totally silent, which meant the learner was unconscious or dead.

Later, Milgram replicated his experiment but instead of having the teacher and learner in separate rooms, the teacher and learner sat side by side. In this case, the teacher was more likely to quit the experiment and refuse to continue the experiment. This part of the experiment says that when people see and hear a person in pain, they are less likely to inflict pain on that person. This is why cyberbullying is so easy and happens more often than traditional bullying, because it is easier than traditional bullying. Bullies do not have to see or hear the pain that they are inflicting on someone else. But the other aspect to all this is that with social media bullying is brought home. Home was a place where many kids could go to avoid bullies from school. Now that space is not safe for them anymore.

Next door to Highland Park, Illinois, where Ferris Bueller and his friends lived is the ultra-affluent and unapologetically haughty community of Lake Forest, Illinois. Robert Redford's 1980 best picture film *Ordinary People*, based on Judith Guest's novel, takes a serious look at the complexities of family, depression, and teen suicide. Conrad Jarrett a teenager is tormented by guilt after his brother Buck dies while they are both sailing on Lake Michigan. Six months after the accident, Conrad attempts suicide and is admitted into a psychiatric hospital.

The film begins after Conrad comes home from the hospital. Conrad goes back to school and struggles to get back to his old life. He has yet to come to terms with his brother's death and blames himself for Buck's death. His mother Beth is not making things any better for him. She too has not come to terms with her son's death and tries to keep a façade that everything is ok. Conrad also feels that his mother cared more about his brother than him and that she is blaming him for his brother's death. Worried that Conrad may attempt suicide again, Conrad's father, Calvin, has him seeing Dr. Berger, a psychiatrist in Highland Park, Illinois. Conrad eventually comes to terms with his brother's death with the help of Dr. Berger. One could easily see in the film that this is a major turning point Conrad's struggle of feeling guilty about his brother's death. Conrad's mother however continues to be cold and distant to him. She feels that Conrad is manipulating his father and the family is being torn apart. There are some awkward scenes in the film, between Conrad and his mother. They try to avoid each other in the house and when they do interact, they seem more like strangers than mom and son.

Another turning point in the film happens in the end. This turning point is often ignored by critics of the novel and film. Calvin, Conrad's father grows up in an orphanage in Detroit. He has an unhappy childhood, but he works hard, goes on to college, and becomes a successful tax attorney. It's difficult for him to understand why his family is so unhappy since they have everything.

At the end of the film, however, Calvin is left to make a difficult life decision. Tensions reach a breaking point between mother and son. Calvin knows that he could side with his wife Beth against their son, but if he does so he risks losing his son to suicide. His other option is to side with his son, who desperately needs him, but if he chooses this option, he risks the chance of losing his wife Beth. He decides to side with his son Conrad. Tells Beth, he no longer loves her. Beth packs her bags and leaves. The film ends with father and son standing side by side in their backyard on a late brisk fall morning while they stare in the distance. It is a difficult decision that Calvin makes. He realizes that his son's life is more important than his marriage.

Rich or poor, every family has issues. For wealthier families, these issues can sometimes be more profound as the case of the Jarrett family in *Ordinary People*. Money can provide a quick solution to a problem, but often it only masks the problem. Kids often bear the brunt when there are problems in the household. We see this in our classroom with kids who are acting up when they are only longing for attention and love that they are not getting at home.

Many parents struggle talking to their kids. A friend of mine told me that the best time for him to talk to his teenage son is in the car to school. He says, "We don't have to look at each other in the car and have those awkward moments. I just drive, look at the road, ask questions and listen to him. I feel we connect best during our drive in the morning." Those talking 15 or 30 minutes in the car make a whole lot of difference to the child. There is no standard teaching manual in being a parent. Most parents learn as they go; often they learn on being a parent from their parents. If they were a product of bad parenting, they a likely to continue that cycle with their own children. I see my former students today go through the wringer when trying to get a teaching job. They may go through a series of two to three interviews, be asked to teach a lesson to a group of students they have never met, go through a background check, provide references, and write a series of essays from why they want to be a teacher to how they would handle a situation in their classroom. This is all fine because we want teachers to be vetted, but anyone can have a child, and many do not know how to raise a child or are provided with basic support to raise that child.

The country of Finland gives expected mothers what is called a "Baby Box." For the last eighty years in Finland, every pregnant woman has been gifted a "Baby Box" by the Finnish government. The box helps a mother and child get through their first year together. The box includes diapers, formula, blankets, snowsuit, thermometer, condoms, and medicines. The box in which the items come in turns into a bassinet. The mother in return is expected to attend a prenatal clinic before her fourth month of pregnancy, about raising her child and on parenting. Similarly, the country of Iceland has redefined what is a family. Icelanders are no longer getting married, at least formerly, and many men and women have children with several partners. Icelanders frown on the use of the term "broken family"; they say instead there is no such thing as broken family, all children are our children to be cared for. Both Iceland and Finland are ranked as one of the best places when it comes to equality for women.

In the previous chapter, we saw Agamemnon sacrifice his daughter for his own personal glory. I said that Agamemnon would not make a good teacher because he lacked empathy. But Agamemnon is also a bad parent because he did not care about his daughter's life. While we also hope that no family experiences what the Jarret family did in *Ordinary People*, many families today experience tragedy, depression, mental illness, and drug abuse. This is something we may not see as teachers, but it is something we need to be aware of if we are to help our students become successful.

## ZOOM PARTIES AND REMOTE LEARNING

When it comes to remote learning, people seem to focus on the inefficiencies of technology or that students do not possess the proper equipment or training to engage in a virtual classroom. Technology is certainly a moving target. It's constantly changing, and more and more people are gaining access to it each year. However, is online or virtual learning the future of education? The Greek philosopher Aristotle once said:

> Man is by nature a social animal; an individual who is unsocial naturally and not accidentally is either beneath our notice or more than human. Society is something that precedes the individual. Anyone who either cannot lead the common life or is so self-sufficient as not to need to, and therefore does not partake of society, is either a beast or a god.

Aristotle understood that humans are wired to interact with other humans and that a Greek god could care less to interact with a mortal human. Online, synchronous, or asynchronous is not the same as face-to-face learning. Would you rather meet your friends in person or over Zoom? Most people I know would want to meet their friends in person.

Many parents today feel that there is too much technology. I overheard a parent say to their kid one day, "We use to go out and meet our friends at coffee shops and bars and restaurants, all you kids do these days is stay home and text your friends." The pandemic has shown us how inefficient technology can be and that children need to interact with one another. During Covid it worked fine, but it can never accomplish the type of learning that occurs in a face-to-face classroom.

Learning is not just about dishing out information. It is about the interaction we have with our students and the relationships we build with them. It's about community and about relationships. The educational historian Jonathan Zimmerman says, "Social distancing is necessary to preserve good health, but it's not good for education. And if you think otherwise, just ask your students. Online instruction might be our new emperor, at least for the moment, but we shouldn't deny what's right in front of our eyes."[23] Are you okay attending religious services online, seeing the Colosseum or Acropolis on Wikipedia, meeting with friends and family on Facetime, or would you rather do all this in person? Technology has always been used in schools. While it has enhanced teaching, it has never transformed it. It is the teachers who have always transformed their classrooms.

"Hey, Teacher, Leave them Kids Alone!" is from Pink Floyd's 1979 song *Another Brick on the Wall*. The music video of the song is of British children in a traditional classroom scolded by their teachers. The song is about the lack of creativity and free expression in the classroom. In Gloria Ladson Billings's well-known book *The Dreamkeepers: Successful Teachers of African American Children*, Billings finds that successful teachers seek excellence, while unsuccessful teachers try to just maintain the status quo.[24] Today each individual student brings his/her diverse experiences into the classroom. As educators, we should welcome this and not scold it as in the Pink Floyd song.

We should also remember that somebody who goes to the best schools could still be very ignorant, and somebody who has no formal education could still be very intelligent. Don Michael Randal who was president of the University of Chicago in the early 2000s once told a story about his mother. His mother had no formal education and Randal said to me, "She was one of the smartest people he ever knew." Randal completed his PhD at Princeton University. For most of his academic career, he specialized in the music of the Middle Ages and the Renaissance, particularly, Arabic music. He remembered his mother working on their family farm in Oklahoma. He said, "She was always digging! I mean always digging." To preoccupy her mind with hard work and the hot Oklahoma sun, Randal's mother was always thinking when she was working. In her house, she had all sorts of books and just about everything. She would read her books and then go off and work and think about what she read and not what she was doing. Surely, she was thinking about other things as well, about her family, perhaps her childhood, or just what to make for dinner that evening. I heard Randel speak about his mother in 2012 in Chicago.

Teaching children to love learning may sound cliché, but once a child learns to love to learn she will continue to want to learn. Learning becomes unlimited to the child. While Randal's mother would be considered uneducated by many because she did not have much of a formal education, she learned to love learning, continued to learn for much of her life, and passed her love of learning to her son Randal.

## NOTES

1. Leavitt, Steven D. and Dubner, Stephen J. (2009). *Freakonomics: A Rogue Economists the Hidden Side of Everything.* New York: William Murrow Paperbacks.

2. Zimmerman, Jonathan. (2002). *Whose America? Culture Wars in the Public Schools.* Cambridge, MA: Harvard University Press, p. 222.

3. Bloom, Alan. (1987). *The Closing of the American Mind.* New York: Simon and Shuster.

4. Brown, Brené. (2010). "The Power of Vulnerability." *TED TALKS.* https://www.ted.com/talks/brene_brown_the_power_of_vulnerability/transcript?language=en

5. Buckley, Madeline. (October, 2017). "Nearly 3,000 People Shot in Chicago So Far this Year." *Chicago Tribune.*

6. Ibid.

7. Alexander City Schools. (2012). *Student/Parent Information Guide and Code of Conduct,* p. 57.

8. Bibb County Board of Education. (2013). *Student Policies,* p. 82.

9. Yates, Eames. (February, 2013). "Paddling in Schools Still Alive and Well in Georgia." *WCTV-TV.*

10. Wm. A. Chaffin, Master, November 10, 1848.

11. CNN November 4, 2008.

12. Coats, Ta-Nehisi. (2015). *Between the World and Me*. New York: Spiegel & Grau, pp. 6–7.

13. Emdin, Christopher. (2016). *For White Folks Who Teach in the Hood . . . And the Rest of Y'all Too: Reality Pedagogy and Urban Education*. Boston, MA: Beacon Press.

14. Gilliam, Walter S. "Early Childhood Expulsions and Suspensions Undermining Our Nation's Most Promising Agent of Opportunity and Social Justice." Robert Wood Johnson Foundation.

15. Washington, Booker T. (1995). *Up From Slavery*. Mineola, NY: Dover Publications, p. 19.

16. Sini, Rozina. (April, 2017). "You are Being Programmed, Former Facebook Executive Warns." *BBC News*. http://www.bbc.com/news/blogs-trending-42322746 Retrieved April 18, 2018.

17. Greenfield, Susan. (2015). *Mind Change: How Digital Technologies Are Leaving Their Mark on Our Brains*. Random House, p. 265.

18. Stockdale, Laura A. et al. (2015). "Emotionally Anesthetized: Media Violence Induces Neural Changes During Emotional Face Processing." *Social Cognitive and Affective Neuroscience*, pp. 1373–1382.

19. Wilson, Gary. (2014). *Your Brain on Porn: Internet Pornography and the Emerging Science of Addiction*. Kent, UK: Commonwealth Publishing, pp. 58–59.

20. American Psychological Association. (2015). *APA Review Confirms Link Between Playing Violent Video Games and Aggression*. http://www.apa.org/news/press/releases/2015/08/violent-video-games.aspx Retrieved June 15, 2018.

21. Gentile, Douglas A. et al. (2017). "Violent Video Games on Salivary Cortisol, Arousal, and Aggressive Thoughts in Children." *Computers in Human Behavior*, pp. 39–43.

22. Hinduja, Sameer and Patchin, Justin W. (2010). "Bullying, Cyberbullying, and Suicide." *Archives of Suicide Research*, 14(3), pp. 206–221.

23. Zimmerman, Jonathan. (2020). "Video Kills the Teaching Star: Remote Learning and the Death of Charisma." *The Chronicle of Higher Education*. https://www.chronicle.com/article/video-kills-the-teaching-star/

24. Ladson-Billings, Gloria. (2009). *The Dreamkeepers: Successful Teachers of African-American Children*. Jossey-Bass.

# Chapter 4

# A Short History of Teachers

Since the beginning of formal schooling in the United States, each generation of teachers has waged a valiant struggle against the injustices in our schools. Some were more evident than others, but all were guided by a sense of righteousness and probity, a quality shared by all good teachers, even today.

Before the establishment of formal schools in the United States, few children received an education. Children who were fortunate enough to receive an education were usually taught by private tutors. This was a tradition adopted from Europe and only children from well-to-do families had access to this type of education.

Beginning in the nineteenth century, some communities opened schools. These schools were supported by fees paid by members of the community. They often favored boys over girls because girls were not expected to receive an education. Most of the teachers in these schools were men, who received no formal training to become teachers. In fact, it was a job given to someone who often had trouble finding work or was seen as incompetent by the community.

By 1850, a prospering American economy, particularly in cities, led to the growth of public schools called Common Schools. With economic prosperity, the teaching profession was transformed from a mostly male-dominated profession to a female one.

The educational historian Donald Warren found that within the last three decades of the nineteenth century, "the number of teachers in the United States more than tripled, from 126,822 to nearly 450,000."[1] Warren found that "in 1870 about two-thirds of American teachers were women . . . and by 1900, three quarters of all teachers were female, as were more than 82 percent in cities with population over 25,000."[2] Many women would leave the home for the first time to become teachers.

As discussed in previous chapters, teachers are put in a special category in most societies. But often we take teachers for granted. We say we value them, that they are important, but fail to support them when they need us most.

Most people today have at some point interacted with a teacher. In fact, it would be unusual if someone didn't. Often the first profession that a child learns about is teaching, and many children want to be teachers when they grow up. While we can't think of a functional society without teachers, historically teachers struggled to be recognized in the United States.

This chapter looks at the lives of several teachers. It is a short history of teachers in the United States. The key figures discussed in the chapter are important because they helped shape the teaching profession. Like many teachers today, these seminal figures, who took it upon themselves to become teachers, dealt with many of the same issues that teachers deal with today: few school resources, low wages, gender, and racial inequality. They are reformers, activists, and feminists, but most importantly, they are individuals who cared about their students.

## BREAKING THE CULT OF TRUE WOMANHOOD

### Willard, Lyon, Beecher, and Anthony

For much of the late eighteenth and nineteenth centuries, men and women lived separate lives. Victorian notions of a "Cult of True Womanhood" defined a woman's role in society.[3] Women were expected to live their lives both inside and outside the home in this way.[4] A strict kingship system identified women as wives, mothers, daughters, and sisters. Their power was limited and rested on their work in their homes. An early decree shows how female teachers were expected to behave in both private and public life.

*Rules for Teachers*

1) You will not marry during the term of your contract.
2) You are not to keep company with men.
3) You must be home during the hours of 8 p.m. and 6 a.m., unless attending a school function.
4) You may not loiter downtown in ice cream stores.
5) You may not travel beyond the city limits unless you have the permission of the chairman of the board.
6) You may not ride in a carriage or automobile with any man unless it is your father or brother.
7) You may not dress in bright colors.
8) You may under no circumstances dye your hair.

9) You must wear at least two petticoats.
10) Your dresses must not be any shorter than 2 inches above the ankle.
11) To keep the schoolhouse neat and clean you must: sweep the floor at least once daily, scrub the floor at least once a week with hot, soapy water, clean the blackboards at least once a day, and start the fire at 7 a.m. so the room will be warm by 8 a.m.[5]

If a teacher married, she was expected to leave her teaching job. Generally, women did not enjoy the same privileges as men. They were viewed as inferior, and they were not expected to receive any formal schooling. In fact, some believed education for women was harmful to their psychology and even biology. But education was more a threat in disrupting the social and gender order of the time. If women received education, it was in basic literacy and numeracy, and they were not allowed to study the same subjects that men did. This injustice against women was nonetheless concealed within the social fabric of American society, and most women were unaware that society was working against them.

In most homes, women were responsible for the everyday operation of the home and estate. Women were dependent on their husbands. They were expected to raise their children and mediate family issues, and nothing more. Early documents describe women as sensitive, pious, caring, and nurturing. Men, on the other hand, were described as rational, practical, and decisive. Defined societal norms excluded women from a life in public. They typically stayed in the home and interacted with other women in their homes.

By the middle of the nineteenth century, education for women became more accepted. But it was in many ways still seen as a way to better prepare women as mothers and wives and not enter the workforce. The teaching profession however helped women break some societal norms. Inevitably, it took women out of their private lives and into the public sphere, challenging traditional notions of the role of women and advocating for women's rights. Several early women helped make significant strides in equal rights through women's work in the teaching profession.

Emma Hart Willard (1787–1850), one of America's first women's rights activists who was also a teacher, describes her early experience teaching children:

> Then I was wont to consider that my first duty as a teacher, required of me that I should labor to make my pupils by explanation and illustration understand their subject, and get them warmed into it, by making them see its beauties and its advantages. During this first part of the process, I talked much more than the pupils were required to do, keeping their attention awake by frequent questions,

requiring short answers from the whole class—for it was ever my maxim, if attention fails, the teacher fails.[6]

For Emma Hart Willard, her experience as a teacher at the age of seventeen was liberating and empowering. She believed her role was greater because she had the ability to change her students' lives.[7] She also understood what most good teachers understood, "If her students failed, she failed."

In 1821, Willard opened the Troy Female Seminary in upstate New York, an all-woman's religious postsecondary school. Women who attended the school were inundated in subjects like history, mathematics, science, history, and geography.[8] The curriculum at Troy Female Seminary was an adapted curriculum used at many all-male schools at the time. Willard believed that women in her school could learn the same subjects that men were learning.[9] Her school was one of the first of its kind in the United States and led to the opening of several other women's postsecondary schools across the country.

Willard was also a philanthropist. She would later write several textbooks and use the proceeds from her textbooks to help educate women in Greece.[10] While Willard helped put some cracks in the glass ceiling for women, education for women and women's work outside the home still had a long way to go.

Like Willard, Mary Lyon (1797–1849) began her career as a teacher at several schools in Massachusetts. For some time, she worked at the Ipswich Female Seminary where she got the idea for her own school for women.[11] In 1837, she founded Mount Holyoke Seminary, with the financial support of a philanthropist who shared her belief in supporting women's education. Like Willard's school, women at Mount Holyoke took classes to those offered at all-male colleges. Lyon is remembered today for telling her students to "go forward, attempt great things, accomplish great things."

Willard and Lyon's work opened the door for women in higher education in the United States. Several women's postsecondary schools were opened in New England and the Mid-Atlantic after Troy Female Academy and Mount Holyoke Seminary. In 1933, Oberlin Collegiate Institute became the first school to admit both women and African Americans. In 1856, the University of Iowa became the first public institution to admit women and by the later part of the nineteenth century, the Sister Colleges of Vassar in New York and Smith and Wellesley in Massachusetts opened their doors to an all-women student body.

Like Willard and Lyon, the social activist and early feminists Catharine Beecher (1800–1878) proposed that teaching was a woman's true profession. She wrote:

The immediate object which has called us together is an enterprise now in progress, the design of which is to educate destitute American children, by the agency of American women. It is an effort which has engaged the exertion of many ladies of various sects, and of all sections in our country, and one which, though commencing in a jumbled way and on a small scale, we believe is eventually to exert a most extensive and saving influence through the nation.[12]

A strict abolitionist, Beecher understood that women could unite around the teaching profession. The profession would help empower women, take them out of their homes, help them organize, and lead them to greater freedoms and toward more rights in America.[13] Beecher campaigned for more women teachers in the frontier and advocated for more teacher training programs to train young women.[14] She helped found three organizations: The Ladies' Society for Promoting Education in the West, the Board of National Popular Education, and the American Women's Educational Association, all of which set out to train new teachers to teach in the West. Beecher proclivity to educating wealthier women differed from Lyon's focus on educating women from more modest social backgrounds.[15] Beecher moreover believed it was the women's duty to her country to be a teacher.

Like Beecher, Susan B. Anthony (1820–1906) (who is best remembered for women's suffrage) worked with teachers to help them gain equal pay. During the 1853 New York City Teachers' Association she advocated that women be allowed to speak in public, which was frowned upon at the time.[16] At the 1857 teacher's convention, Anthony proposed a resolution that would allow African Americans admission into public schools and colleges.[17] Her ideas were radical for the time, and many felt threatened by them, but she was forward thinking and sought change for the marginalized.

During much of the nineteenth and twentieth centuries, teachers were paid less than other professionals, and women teachers were even paid less than their male counterparts. There are even cases as early as the 1840s of school boards firing teachers to help keep salaries low. But as the profession began to grow, teachers demanded more rights and higher pay. At the same time, however, not all women would have the same rights. Black women in the South were still under the brutal practice of slavery and in the North black women did not enjoy the same rights as white women.

## BLACK WOMEN IN WHITE PETTICOATS

In the African American community, teachers historically have enjoyed a high level of respect and admiration. Indeed, in some black communities, teachers are regarded more favorably than other professions. This is partly because teachers are seen to be most responsive and sympathetic to the needs of the community. African American women had their own reasons for becoming teachers. It was perhaps to escape poverty, find freedom, or help uplift their community after slavery. The historian Linda M. Perkins argues that during much of the nineteenth and early twentieth centuries,

> for white women, education served as a vehicle for developing homemaker skills, for reinforcing the role of wife and mother, and a milieu for finding a potential husband. For black women education served as an avenue for the improvement of their race or race uplift.[18]

Like white women, gender-role stereotyping eased African American women into teaching. The struggle to become teachers for African American women was nonetheless more difficult than their white counterparts. While educational opportunities were expanding for white women during the middle part of the nineteenth century, education for African Americans was acutely limited.

Before the Civil War in 1865, education for slaves was illegal in the South, and in the North, education for African Americans was vastly limited. Horace Mann of Massachusetts who led the struggle for public education largely left African Americans out of his vision of public schooling in the United States.

Major shifts to the education of blacks began as early as 1840, through the courageous efforts of a little black girl and her fastidious father. One morning in the early fall of 1840, Sarah Roberts woke up for her first day of school in Boston. Like most children that day, she washed her face, got dressed in her new school uniform, ate her breakfast, and got her shoes on to walk to school.

Her father Benjamin Roberts was going to walk Sarah to school. As they walked together, Mr. Roberts assured his daughter everything was going to be okay, that she would make a lot of new friends and learn a lot of new things in school. But, when they arrived at the school, the headmaster came to the door and asked them to leave. Bewildered, they continued to walk down the street to the next school, but once they reached the door of that school they were once again asked to leave.

The story of Sarah Roberts's first day of school, while fictionalized to a certain extent, leads to the desegregation of schools in Boston and much of the North. Sarah's father, Benjamin Roberts, simply wanted his daughter to go to a better school that was near his home. His application to get his daughter into a neighborhood school was rejected. He subsequently filed a legal suit against the city of Boston. African American children were restricted to attend only two schools in Boston, both of which were segregated.

In *Roberts v. City of Boston*, the Massachusetts Supreme Court ruled against Sarah Roberts, but in 1855, a law was passed prohibiting segregated schools in Massachusetts. Other states followed suit and segregated schools were gradually abolished in much of New England and the North. The South however would remain segregated until the landmark *Brown v. Board of Education* decision of 1955, and even after this decision, the U.S. government had to intervene to force schools to desegregate.

Historians see the Sarah Roberts' precedent legal case as the first pivotal step to the desegregation of schools in the United Sates.[19] The case undoubtedly opened the door for a fair and equitable education for all Americans. However, unlike the experience of white women, the rooted racism of nineteenth-century America actively worked to deny most African American women access to the teaching profession. If they became teachers, they were expected to stay in their communities and work with black children. They were also expected to follow the prescribed social norms of a woman's role in American society, which further limited opportunities for them.

In 1863, Abraham Lincoln issued the Emancipation Proclamation which declared the end of slavery in the United States. In 1865, the Civil War ended, and the Thirteenth Amendment was ratified to the Constitution, which gave full citizenship to all slaves.

The training and preparation of members of the African American community were supported through the establishment of Historically Black Colleges by the Freedmen's Bureau Act of 1868.[20] But *Jim Crow* and even the establishment of exclusive Black Colleges only necessitated segregation in the South. Many wealthy whites funded black colleges to assure that African Americans did not attend white colleges and white public schools. In many of the black colleges (a grievance that W. E. B. Du Bois often expressed), African Americans were limited to vocational training. "Education must not simply teach work-it must teach life," Du Bois famously told graduates at Fisk University.[21] For Du Bois, if the community was to prosper it needed to learn what white people were learning.

In the North, many whites opened schools for blacks, but many African Americans complained it was only to train them to serve in subordinate roles and to work for whites. While many African Americans were suspicious of white intentions, they wanted good schools and competent teachers for their children. They also felt that black teachers were best suited to teach black children and that education and schooling would help the community heal from the savage and debilitating bonds of slavery.

According to a study conducted by W. E. B. Du Bois, five years after the end of the Civil War in the South, there were about 7,000 black teachers and 250,000 black students, which was roughly about thirty-six students per teacher.[22] The issue was not only large class size for black schools but the conditions in which many black children were living: inadequate living quarters, no running water, and extreme poverty.

Missionary groups traveled South to help the newly freed slave communities. The newly freed slaves quickly embraced the opportunity to an education and saw education as a way out of poverty. The 1870 *Report of the Commissioner of Education on the Improvement of Public Schools in the District of Columbia* noted that many African Americans in the South were enthusiastic about receiving an education and wanted their children to go to school.[23]

The teaching profession quickly caught on in the African American community. In fact, it was a profession most African American women would go into. By the early part of the twentieth century, three out of four professional African American women worked as teachers.[24] After slavery was abolished in the South, many African American men and women from the North traveled to the South to teach newly freed black children. They believed that they needed to give back to their community and that their greatest impact would be teaching children from their community.[25]

One such teacher was Charlotte Forten (1837–1914). Forten was the first African American woman from the North to travel to the South and help educate recently emancipated black children.[26]

Born in Philadelphia in 1837, Forten came from a well-known African American family from the North.[27] Her grandfather was a successful businessman, which allowed her to go to school in Massachusetts.[28] She later began teaching in Salem, Massachusetts, where she was the first African American woman hired to be a teacher. She describes an invitation she received from Mrs. Shepard to teach in Salem schools:

> Week before last I had a letter from Many Shepard asking me to come on and take charge of S.C.'s classes during the summer, as she was obliged to go away. How gladly I accepted, you, dear A., may imagine. I had been longing so for a breath of New England air; for a glimpse of the sea, for a walk over our good hills. . . . We left Philadelphia on Tuesday, the 10th; stopped a little while in New York. . . . Then took the evening boat, and reached here on Wednesday morn. Mrs. Ives gave us the most cordial welcome; and we felt immediately at home.[29]

Forten, however, eventually became restless in Salem. She felt that she could do more as a teacher elsewhere and work with those who needed her the most. By the later part of 1862, she embarked to St. Helena, an island located off the coast of South Carolina, where she joined Laura Towne, a well-known American abolitionist and educator.

Many of the children Forten taught at St. Helena spoke only Gullah, a West African language. They were the descendants of early slaves brought to the island from West Africa in the sixteenth century.[30] Because they were isolated on St. Helena their language and culture had been preserved.[31] Forten saw the

Gullah as hard-working and industrious. She also noticed that she needed to use a different teaching approach for the children at St. Helena than the one she was used to in Salem.

In 1864, Forten wrote an article in the *Atlantic Monthly* on her experience at St. Helena titled "Life on the Sea Islands." The article exposed many Americans not only to the thinly known culture of the Gullah but also to the conditions of the school that Forten taught. Below is an excerpt from her article:

> I never saw children so eager to learn, although I had had several years' experience in New England schools. Coming to school is a constant delight and recreation to them. They come here as other children go to play. The older ones, during the summer, work in the fields from early morning until eleven or twelve o'clock, and then come into school, after their hard toil in the hot sun, as bright and as anxious to learn as ever. The majority learn with wonderful rapidity. Many of the grown people are desirous of learning to read. It is wonderful how a people who have so long crushed to the earth, so most degraded negroes of the South,-can have so great a desire for knowledge, and such a capability for attaining it.[32]

Forten in many ways was the first teacher to use an Afro-centric approach in her teaching. She taught her students to feel proud of their history and heritage by teaching them how their ancestors had contributed to the world and that they were not just descendants of slaves but that their ancestors were kings and queens.[33] Forten also showed her students the intellectual potential that they could achieve and succeed in life through a good education.

When Forten arrived at St. Helena, she found herself facing challenges with her students far beyond the scope of her experiences in Salem, challenges that could not simply be solved through teaching her students to read and write. Her students were living in former slave quarters, without running water or clean clothes and had limited access to food. Despite these challenges, she continued to believe in her students. Although Forten came from a well-to-do family, her privileged status in the North clearly provided her access to the teaching profession and other resources unavailable to blacks in the South. After teaching at St. Helena, Forten moved to Washington, DC. She married Francis Grimke, a minister. She continued to support equal rights for blacks up until her death in 1914.

Other African American women would follow in Forten's footsteps. After the Civil War, Washington, DC, became a Mecca for former slaves from the South seeking opportunities. The Washington, DC, school system also provided significantly more funding to their segregated schools than in other parts of the South.[34] It was also easier and safer for a former slave to travel to Washington, DC, than North to New England.

Anna Julia Cooper (1858–1964) would become the first former female slave to receive a PhD in the United States.[35] Born into slavery in North Carolina in 1858, she would eventually move to Washington, DC, where she would attend DC's segregated color schools and work as a teacher for more than sixty years.[36]

Few African Americans during Cooper's time received an education beyond elementary school. It was also uncommon for an African American woman to receive a high school education. W. E. B. Du Bois had to go to Germany to complete his PhD because most American universities refused to admit him for fear that it would scare their donors.

In 1821, Cooper began attending Oberlin College. The college was fervently abolitionist and sympathetic to the African American cause. After completing her degree at Oberlin, Cooper began teaching at M Street High School in Washington, DC, and in 1901, she became principal of the school. While principal, Cooper worked with her students to help them get into college. Oberlin also became a popular feeder college for many M Street graduates.

It is in Washington, DC, that Cooper developed a friendship with Charlotte Forten and worked with her on the equal rights of African Americans. Cooper later moved to Paris and completed her PhD at the University of Paris in 1924. Her dissertation, on the historical topic of the Haitian Slave Revolt during and French Revolutions became well-known among historians of her time.

While Cooper did not write much about her experiences in Europe, other African American writers who traveled to Europe reflected later that they felt more accepted in Europe than in their own country. In fact, many African Americans did not return to the United States after visiting Europe because they felt they were respected there more than in America. Cooper, however, felt that her calling was to help her community in her own country. She returned to the United States and dedicated her life to the education of black children.

Like Cooper, Fanny Jackson Coppin (1837–1913) was born as a slave. In her early teens, she was purchased by her aunt and worked as a domestic servant.[37] She saved some of her earnings and left to attend Rhode Island State Normal School and Oberlin College.[38] At Oberlin, she taught courses to freed slaves from the South. After graduating from Oberlin in 1865, Coppin began teaching at the Institute for Colored Youth (ICY) in Philadelphia. She later became principal of the school and like Cooper encouraged her students to further their education.

By the late nineteenth century, three-quarters of the black teachers in Philadelphia were ICY graduates.[39] Many went to the South to teach. Students at ICY learned to draw, make maps, and develop other skills to work in industrial fields. Coppin even hired a doctor to teach students about health, hygiene, and sexually transmitted diseases.[40]

Like Booker T. Washington, Coppin believed that her students needed jobs and that vocational training was important for this to happen.[41] She created an Industrial Department at ICY and established a Women's Industrial Exchange to help young women find work in the industrial fields.[42] By the later part of the nineteenth century, Booker T. Washington's vision of industrial or vocational training for African Americans became popular.

Washington believed that the community needed training in hand and work, and it was for later generations to be trained in the humanities and arts. In 1881, Coppin married Rev. Levi J. Coppin, a prominent African American minister, and together they continued to serve their community. She retired from ICY in 1902 at age sixty-five but continued working with black students.

While it was an uphill battle for white women to receive an education, it was more of a herculean task for African American women to receive an education and become teachers. Both groups nonetheless struggled to do so. Later they would unite with a shared interest and a common goal for equal rights for all women. In the meantime, America was expanding westward, it was America's destiny to settle the West, even if it was at the expense of America's indigenous peoples. New towns and communities sprung up. Teachers were in need to help "tame" the West and educate the children of a rapidly growing westward population.

## CIVILIZERS AND MISSIONARIES

Frederick Turner Jackson's "Frontier Thesis" fits well into the story of women teachers moving westward. Jackson believed that the success of the United States was tied to westward expansion.[43] Later it would be called "Manifest Destiny" or America's destiny to settle the West. Jackson however largely left women out of his Thesis and was even hesitant to credit women for their contribution to the West. Historians moreover portrayed women as reluctant to move westward and only do so because they are led by their "industrious" and "adventurous" husbands and fathers.[44]

But the story of women teachers moving westward is very different. In this story, teachers are the ones who are adventurous and courageous and not men. The West allowed women to travel and see parts of the country that most Americans would never see. Teaching gave women a sense of independence and a feeling of empowerment that was not as accessible to them in other parts of the country. Many women in the West found no need to marry and have families of their own. It is no surprise that so many American feminists and women's rights advocates were teachers who taught in the West.

But it was also for the love of teaching and children that many women traveled West to work as teachers.

Although women teachers were not equal to men in the West, they did not need to conform to the same restrictive standards set forth for women in the eastern part of the country. The West was an unsettled territory, and the same rules that governed much of the rest of the country did not apply there. Moreover, most women teachers did not have to rely on men to support them but developed instead elaborate support networks with other women. Individually and collectively these women responded to inequality by relying on themselves and working together to survive and succeed in a territory that was new, dangerous, and foreign to them.

The nineteenth century was an exciting time in America. The country was optimistic, and people were looking forward to the future. The United States was expanding across continental North America, and better systems in transportation and communication were connecting people. While cities like Boston, Philadelphia, and New York were already established, new opportunities were found in the West. More states were also joining the Union. California in 1850, Oregon in 1859, Nevada in 1864, Nebraska in 1867, Colorado in 1876, South and North Dakota, Montana, and Washington in 1889, Wyoming and Idaho in 1890, and Utah in 1896.

As new towns sprang up, a surge in population growth occurred to help accommodate new industries in lumber and mining. While there were settlers headed West prior to the Civil War, the most rapid migration occurred after the Homestead Act in 1862 and the completion of the transcontinental railroad in 1869. The Homestead Act allowed settlers to claim 160 acres of land for free and to farm that land. The American economy was booming, and money was being invested throughout the country. As towns and cities began to grow and as more and more families moved West, teachers were also needed to accommodate the children living in these communities.

The schools in which they taught varied by location, they could be in a rural town, small city, or even a reservation. Most schools were large wooden cabin-like structures with framed glass windows. The buildings themselves were open and stale and looked more like they were meant for storage or for livestock than for teaching children.

Teachers, mostly women, began arriving West as early as the 1840s to teach the children of pioneers. In her book *The Duty of American Women to Their Country*, Catharine Beecher encouraged women to travel West and serve as teachers, because she believed it was a woman's duty.[45] Today the schoolmarm image of the teacher, prim, strict, brisk, and proper in manner is most associated with the frontier schoolteacher. In John Steinbeck's famous novel *East of Eden* which takes place in Salinas, California, during the settlement of California, Steinbeck describes teachers as follows:

In the country the repository of art and science was the school, and the teacher shielded and carried the torch of learning and beauty. The schoolhouse was the meeting place for music, for debate. The polls were set in the schoolhouse for elections . . . the teacher was not only an intellectual paragon and social leader, but also a matrimonial catch of the countryside.[46]

Teachers had a special status in the West because communities had to rely on them more than in other parts of the country. Out of all the work that women were engaged in in the West, women teachers were viewed as being the most intellectually curious and even better educated than their male counterparts.

Between 1870 and 1900, illiteracy rates in the United States dropped from 20 percent to 10.7 percent.[47] Much of this is attributed to teachers' work in the West. During this same period, the annual salary of teachers almost doubled from $189.00 annually to $325.00.[48] Teachers were in high demand during this period, especially in the West, and communities were willing to pay to get good teachers. The Colorado school population, which was one of the fastest-growing states during westward expansion, grew from 4,387 in 1870 to 117,555 in 1900.[49] With the growth of the student population, more teachers were needed. While most teachers taught white children in fast-growing towns and cities, some felt their calling was to teach Indian children on reservations.

One such teacher was Elaine Goodale Eastman (1863–1953). After the Civil War, there was a strong desire to educate Native American children. Elaine Goodale Eastman grew up in New England and felt her calling was to teach out West. Many Indian children attended boarding schools far from their families. Eastman began teaching in one of these schools in New England. But these schools were controversial during Eastman's time. David Wallace Adams says:

Thus, a high percentage of [Indian] children were destined to have a boarding school experience. Slowly at first, and then with ever increasing momentum, the idea was gaining force that Indian children needed to be removed from their tribal homes for the assimilationists promise to be realized.[50]

The schools were really there to assimilate Indian children into mainstream white culture. After teaching at these schools, Eastman moved to the Dakota Territories (now North and South Dakota) to work as a teacher on a reservation. She describes her experience after arriving at a reservation school as follows, "Every morning a rag of white fluttered from the cabin roof to indicate that school was open. Then pupils came and went at their pleasure with little attempt at order and discipline. They did learn something nonetheless."[51] Eastman later opens a day school on the Sioux reservation and some years later becomes supervisor of Indian Education for the Two Dakotas. As a supervisor, she fights hard against the separation of children from their families and homes to attend boarding schools. But the schools she runs also work toward assimilating Indian children. Like many women of her time, Eastman's upper New England background surely provided her the opportunity to become a teacher and to travel West. While her calling may have been misguided, it was without a doubt well-intended. She is guilty of the popular misguided notion of the time to "civilize" or "tame" Native American groups. This was not only happening in the United States but in Africa, Asia, and Latin America, as Europeans sought to assimilate peoples living under their colonial rule. This was no different in the United States as white culture dominated the North American continent and imposed their will on indigenous groups.

Many of the children in Eastman's school, like the black children in the South discussed earlier in this chapter, suffered from extreme poverty. Indian reservations were typically on the least arable lands, and the schools had very little resources. Many white Americans had found black slaves to be valuable for their labor, Indians, on the other hand, were viewed as savages, and for many white Americans, it was better that they were eradicated or isolated than assimilated into mainstream white American society.

For Eastman, assimilation was about survival for the native peoples because she feared if they were not, they would be killed. The mistreatment of native indigenous groups in the United States is perhaps one of the worst cases of inhumanity in modern world history. The rest of the world was aware of this. When the Ottoman ambassador was confronted by an American ambassador in 1915 about reports of mass killings of Armenian, Greek, and other minorities in the Ottoman Empire, he replied back to the American ambassador, "And what about the Indians."

When the first Europeans set foot on the New World, they were aided by deadly biological weapons. Smallpox and other diseases carried by Europeans would kill off most of America's native groups. In his famous book *Guns, Germs and Steel: The Fates of Human Societies*, Jared Diamond says, "For instance, the Indian population of Hispaniola declined from around 8 million, when Columbus arrived in A.D. 1492, to zero by 1535."[52] The decimation of Native American peoples, whether intended or unintended, killed millions of people. It also fueled slavery and the slave trade as the demand for labor increased.

By the late nineteenth century, industrialization was also demanding more workers to help fuel a rapidly growing American industrial economy. Most of these workers would come from parts of Europe that were not familiar to most Americans. Their religious beliefs, language, and cultural practices were different from the earlier European groups that had settled in America three centuries before. Many of these new immigrants came with their families and would help transform schooling and education in the United States.

## INDUSTRIAL AND IMMIGRANT TEACHERS

In 1903, Adele Marie Shaw, a New York City public school teacher, wrote the following:

> No other municipality [New York City] had even to meet a problem so difficult, so peculiar, and at the same time so all-embracing. With eighty-five percent of its population foreign or of foreign parentage; its salvation dependent upon the conversion of a daily arriving cityful of Russians, Turks, Austro-Hungarians, Sicilians, Greeks, Arabs into good Americans; its ideals; its present effort weighted with the ignorance and corruption of the past, the city has a problem of popular education that is staggering.[53]

By the turn of the nineteenth century, there is a growth of public education in the United States. Much of the century saw vast numbers of immigrants arrive in the United States. More schools and more teachers were needed to help educate these new arrivals. American cities like New York, Baltimore, Boston, Chicago, Milwaukee, and St. Louis were all in need of workers to fill factory jobs.[54] Industrialization, immigration, modernization, and a growing American economy demanded workers to help sustain American economic prosperity.[55] The social historian Paula S. Fass writes:

> Decade after decade in the late nineteenth century, vast numbers of immigrants arrived at American ports, three-fourths of them at New York. Between 1860 and 1890, thirteen and one half million new immigrants arrived. In the first three decades of the twentieth century, nineteen million more made their way to the United States. Between 1890 and 1920, immigrants and their children formed between one-half and three-fourths of the population of cities like Cleveland, Milwaukee, Boston, San Francisco, and St. Louis.[56]

To help accommodate these new arrivals, public school expenditures rose from $69 million in 1870 to $149 million in 1890.[57] Enrollment in public schools also increased. In 1870, there were 7.6 million students from K-12 and by 1880 there were 12.7 million.[58] The United States lead the world in universal education, and American schools became the greatest symbol of democracy in the world.

Most of these new arrivals settled in industrialized cities. Out of the 22 million people that settled in the United States between 1870 and 1930, 3 million were children. Schools quickly shifted their attention from the 3 Rs (Reading, Writing, and Arithmetic) to teaching English and U.S. civics.

Adult education classes were also offered to help assimilate and train immigrant adults. Schooling however was limited for six to eight years so children could begin working by age twelve. By 1910, 2 million children held jobs and preferred to work than go to school. In Chicago, Jane Addams, who was sometimes critical of teacher unions, was a zealot when it came to children's rights. She helped organize to get children back in school and out of factories. What she is most remembered for today and what got her the Nobel Peace Prize.

Today millions of visitors visit Ellis Island in New York City each year. Ellis Island was the first stop for many immigrants between the late nineteenth and early twentieth centuries.

Give me your tired, your poor,
your huddled masses yearning to breathe free,
The wretched refuse of your teeming shore.
Send these, the homeless, tempest-tossed to me,
I lift my lamp beside the golden door!

Reads the inscription below the Statue of Liberty. A symbol of immigration to the United States. For many though, Ellis Island was less about welcoming new immigrants and more about limiting the number of immigrants from certain parts of the world.

Prior to the end of the American Civil War, there were few immigration restrictions to the United States. There was no comprehensive immigration policy or even a federal department that processed new immigrants. Most came to the United States freely from England and other parts of Western Europe. There were certainly others who were forced on America's shores as slaves.

America was very different before the Civil War. It was not the culturally diverse America we see today. Most Americans were white and Protestant. You could imagine a school classroom in 1870 filled with children who all pretty much looked the same. Many of these children could probably trace their ancestry somewhere in Europe.

By the nineteenth century, cities began to grow. More factories were built and workers were needed to help fuel this growth. People moved to America's industrial cities to find work.

They came from Ireland, Italy, Greece, Russia, and other parts of Europe. They also came from the southern United States, many were recently free slaves, while others were rural farmers displaced from this new industrial economy. America was to provide these new transplants a better life, a chance to succeed, and an opportunity for a better education for their children. This was the American dream for many during this time.

Most of these new arrivals like the Irish were Catholic. They were discriminated against for their beliefs, customs, and even the way they dressed and looked. Take the political cartoon from 1890 (figure 4.1).

The cartoon is titled, "The Inevitable Result to the American Workingman of Unrestricted Immigration."[59] It was published in the weekly humor magazine *Judge* in 1890 and shows a poor, swarthy, and disheveled immigrant taking food off the table of a white working American. The cartoon says to those viewing it, be wary, these immigrants will take your jobs and food from your table.

Fear tactics like these were usually used for political purposes, and certainly added to anti-immigrant feelings. One gets a sense of early antagonisms between immigrants and nativist groups in Martin Scorsese's 2002 film *Gangs of New York*. The film takes place in the 1860s in the Five Points District of New York City where large numbers of Irish and Catholic immigrants are making New York City their home.

Many nativists (earlier European immigrants to settle in America) see these new immigrants as a threat. William "Bill the Butcher" Cutting (played

THE INEVITABLE RESULT TO THE AMERICAN WORKINGMAN OF INDISCRIMINATE IMMIGRATION.

**Figure 4.1   The Inevitable Result to the American Workingman** . . . *Source:* The Judge Magazine.

by Daniel Day-Lewis) is a powerful Protestant Anti-Catholic gang leader. In a sadistic way, Cutting takes pleasure in terrorizing new immigrants. Cutting meets an Irish immigrant who he takes a likening to, named Amsterdam Vallon (played by Leonardo Di Caprio). At one point in the film, Cutting belittles Vallon's Irish-Catholic background. He says to him, "On the Seventh Day the Lord rested, but before that he did, he took a squat over the side of England and what came out of him . . . was Ireland. No offense son." This was the feeling many nativists had about Catholic and Irish immigrants. But the public schools also added to an anti-Catholic and anti-Irish sentiment.

School textbooks were filled with comments that dehumanized and derided many immigrant groups. "The Irish are passionate, ignorant vain and superstitious" read one textbook. Catholics were also seen to be loyal to the Pope and not America and they could never be trusted.

The debate of religion in American schools is not new and the separation of church and state was tested as soon as new immigrants, most of them Catholic, began emigrating to America. Catholics felt that Protestantism was pushed on their children in public schools. Common Protestant prayers were used in schools and children read from the *King James Bible*, known to Catholics as the *Protestant Bible*. Many Catholics did not send their children to school because they felt that their children would be converted into Protestantism or feel ashamed about their Irish and Catholic heritage and upbringing.

Today there are many who advocate for prayer in school. But the question is why should schools favor one religion over another? Bishop John Hughes asked for a portion of monies that went to public schools to go to private religious schools. Hughes said:

> The children of foreigners, found in great numbers in our populous cities . . . are too often deprived of the advantages of our system of public education, in consequence of prejudices arising from difference of language or religion. It ought never to be forgotten that the public welfare is as deeply concerned in their education as in that of our own children. I do not hesitate therefore to recommend the establishment of schools in which they may be instructed by teachers speaking the same language with themselves, and professing the same faith.[60]

While Hughes made a convincing case, his proposal was turned down because it would open the door for all religious groups to seek government monies for their own schools, which would threaten the public school system in New York City.

While Hughes's dream of a Catholic school system supported by public funds was denied, he was still able to create one of the largest religiously based school system in the United States. Most Catholic schools were opened in cities where most of the Catholic immigrants lived. The teachers in these schools were usually nuns who were paid very little and taught more as a service to the Church than as a career.

Elizabeth Ann Seton, who would become America's first native-born saint, started the Sisters of Charity, an order that opened separate parochial schools for families of poor and wealthy girls in several American cities. A robust Catholic University system was also created throughout the country, and today many of these universities are some of the best in the world.

According to one report, there were 1.2 million children attending Catholic schools in 1910.[61] The number of teachers teaching in these schools was 31,000 with 8 in 10 being women.[62] If you grew up in a city like Boston, Chicago, Milwaukee, or New York, you could easily feel the impact that the Catholic school system had on your city. Many Catholics and non-Catholics attended Catholic schools and children who attended an elementary Catholic school ended up attending a Catholic high school and Catholic college and university. Catholics usually identified by the parish they attended rather than their neighborhoods. Catholic schools also became a good alternative, and for many, they were better than the public schools.

Public education also demanded more schools and more teachers. In many American cities, new school buildings were built. In most cases, rural towns continued to use the same school buildings they had been using since the early 1800s. The new school buildings that were built were imposing structures that looked more like factories than schools. The brick-and-mortar school buildings of Boston, Chicago, New York, and Milwaukee could be up to three stories tall with up to 20-foot ceilings, giant wide windows, heavy wooden doors, and large smokestacks. The wood detail was typically the main interior feature of the buildings.

Classrooms were almost floor to ceiling with blackboards, and the classrooms were large enough to fit thirty-five to forty students comfortably. These buildings were a radical break from those built during Horace Mann's time. They symbolized industrialization and state-regulated education. They were utilitarian and meant to be efficient.

Mary Antin's *Promised Land* describes her experience as an immigrant student in public schools in the late 1800s. Antin was born into a poor Jewish family from Russia in 1881.[63] She moved to Massachusetts with her mother and siblings in 1884 where her father had already relocated three years earlier. Antin attributed her good writing to her teachers, specifically Miss Dillingham who worked vigorously to help her learn English. Antin's book the *Promised Land* which was published in 1912 helped dispel fears about new immigrants. It humanized the immigrant and gave a picture that the immigrant was no different than other Americans. While Antin appreciated her teachers, she also understood that she was being assimilated into school. The social historian John Bodnar writes:

> Public schools and educational officials, of course, were always interested in using the classroom to inculcate American values and beliefs in the foreign-born and having them abandon their former traits and beliefs which were often perceived to be strange, often radical, and simply undesirable.[64]

Some groups resisted assimilation by opening their own schools. While Catholic schools sought to preserve the Catholic faith and its traditions, other groups like the Greeks and Jews opened schools with the goal of preserving their language and culture as well as their religious traditions. Many of these schools were successful in doing so. The Greek immigrant historian Theodore Saloutos writes, "Emphasis was placed on establishing Greek schools, where young people could be instructed in the traditional faith and language."[65] For immigrant groups, like the Greeks, assimilation was a threat, it meant becoming lost within the diverse cultural milieu of the United States.[66] Because they feared assimilation, the Greek Orthodox Church and Greek American organizations such as The American Hellenic Educational Progressive Association (AHEPA) and wealthy benefactors funded Greek schools. Teachers were even brought from Greece to teach in these schools.[67] Children in the schools learned to speak Greek and the schools were one of the most successful bilingual private school systems in the United States.[68]

While many new immigrants were trying to navigate through American social and cultural life, it was in urban America in the late nineteenth and early twentieth centuries that one could find a rich cultural diversity, which could only be found in American cities. It was moreover a challenge for teachers to teach up to fifty students in a classroom. Many of these students brought to the classroom their own language, traditions, and experiences. More than ten different languages could be spoken in one classroom. In some neighborhoods schools in Chicago and other cities in the United States, this is still true. Instead of Bohemian, German, Spanish, Swedish, Italian, Greek, Czech, Russian, Polish, Yiddish, and Serbo-Croatian, children speak Arabic, Somali, Pashtun, Urdu, Hindi, Kyrgyz, Mandarin, Cantonese, Korean, and Vietnamese. Teachers today are dealing with many of the same issues that they dealt with in the past, but we have teachers now trained to teach English language learners as well as learners who are challenged in other ways.

The normal schools helped better prepare teachers to teach these new-comers. Normal schools were typically two-year teacher training programs, and after completing the program, many teachers found work teaching in America's urban public schools.

Marguerite Renner's study on Pittsburgh Public Schools found a rampant culture of nepotism and corruption in teacher hiring.[69] Teaching jobs were often awarded to a relative of a politician or someone who was politically connected.[70] Often interviews for teaching positions were never conducted.[71] This did not only occur in Pittsburgh but in other cities like Chicago where patronage politics was widespread throughout the city and suburbs. City aldermen often gave jobs to family members or political supporters who had no training to be teachers. There were cases in Chicago where so-called teachers were on the ghost payroll of a school.[72] Thomas J. Gradel, Dick Simpson, and Andris Zenellis write:

> The possibility for corruption and its persistence can also be explained by Chicago's large immigrant population which made it easier for the political machine to grow in power. Millions of Irish, German, Jewish, and Slavic settled in cities of America and these groups had difficulty getting jobs. The immigrants would come to local officials for housing and work thus turning public office into the market for jobs, contracts, and a place to reward "friends."[73]

To help curb corruption, such as ghost pay-rolling, officials forced teachers to sign in and out on timecards. Even today Chicago Public School (CPS) teachers are required to sign in and out on an online time-reporting system called Kronos (*Greek* for time) used to track employee hours even though teachers are salaried employees.

Julia Richman (1855–1912) is perhaps the best-known teacher who taught immigrant children in the late nineteenth century. She was born in New York City to a Jewish family in 1855.[74] In 1870, she enrolled in New York Normal College (later Hunter College) and after graduating returned to New York City to teach in its public schools. She was only seventeen years old when she began teaching and wanted to teach in the school system that she attended. In 1884, she became principal at P.S. 77 and served as principal at that school for nearly nineteen years.[75] In 1903, she was promoted to district superintendent for schools in the Lower East Side of New York City. She was responsible for more than 23,000 students. Many of the schools in her district were attended by immigrant children who did not speak English.

While in this position, she organized separate classes for mentally and physically challenged children. She also opened separate schools for children with delinquency problems. She introduced physical examinations for students and began a program of school lunches for low-income children. She cowrote a series of six textbooks and trained her counselors to advise students who dropped out on how to find a job. During the annual meeting of the National Educational Association, she presented a paper on the immigrant child. In the paper, she wrote:

Ours is a nation of immigrants. The citizen voter of today was yesterday an immigrant child. Tomorrow he may be a political leader. Between the alien of today and the citizen of tomorrow stands the school, and upon the influence exerted by the school depends the kind of citizen the immigrant will become.[76]

She was passionate about educating immigrant children because she herself was the child of immigrants. She also reminded immigrant Americans, as well as the sons and daughters of immigrants to not forget their own struggles and how education helped them succeed in America. In 1906, she moved into the "Teachers House," which was a place where principals, teachers, and social workers met to discuss how to improve New York City Public Schools. In 1912, she traveled to Europe but fell ill and died in Paris. She was only fifty-six years old but had contributed significantly to reforming public education in America.

With an increasing immigrant population and more formal training of teachers, teachers began to raise their voices for changes in the teaching profession. School administrators were often seen as out of touch with the needs of students. Teachers saw themselves as dug in the trenches, working each day with students, knowing their needs as well as what was best for their students in their classrooms. It is no surprise today that many teachers know their students just as much as a parent knows her child because teachers spend just as much time if not more with their students.

## PROGRESSIVE EDUCATORS, SCHOOL REFORMERS, AND LABOR SLUGGERS

Industrialization changed the way people lived and worked. Schooling was not immune to this change. At the intellectual center of the debate on how to transform schools to meet the needs of the industrial child was the American philosopher and educator John Dewey. Dewey said, "If we teach today's students as we taught yesterday's, we rob them of tomorrow." Dewey today is perhaps the most influential educational thinker of the twentieth century. He is also deeply tied to what is called the progressive movement in education. A Vermont native, Dewey was trained as a philosopher. He advocated a teaching approach that centered on the child. This approach would later be called experiential learning or "learning by doing."

Prior to Dewey's ideas, the way teachers taught was mainly through a teacher-centered approach or direct instruction. Students typically sat behind their desks, usually quietly as their teacher lectured to them. Students were expected to take notes and listen. A quiet classroom meant it was a good classroom. But few considered how the student processed the information that was given to them.

Dewey understood that kids had very creative minds and they could find ways to preoccupy or distract their brains when they got bored. For Dewey, to allow students to express their learning, engage the child, keep their minds active, and make teaching fun were important. Dewey essentially came up with the idea that it was not about the teacher, but it was about the student and that it was important to engage the child during a lesson if you expected the child to retain information.

On the campus of the University of Chicago, Dewey opened the Laboratory School to test his ideas on teaching and learning. Teachers were trained to focus on their students' individual needs and not the entire class. They also considered their students' interests when designing their lessons. Teaching was made fun with field trips, learning by play activities, and subjects were brought to life by applying them to a child's life.[77]

There are old photos of children at the Laboratory School designing a sailboat, spinning wool, planting and taking care of a garden, or just running around on Midway Park, "Make every working man a scholar and every scholar a working man" was one of Dewey's mottos at the Laboratory School.

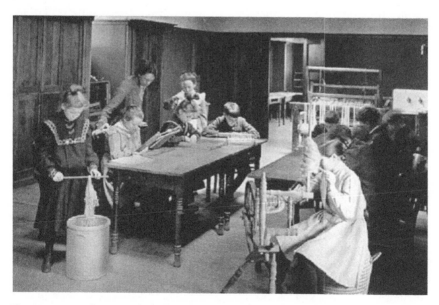

**Figure 4.2 Students at the Laboratory School.** *Source:* Courtesy of University of Chicago.

Classroom at Dewey's Lab School. Students are learning to spin and dye wool. The Photo is courtesy University of Chicago. Circa 1930.

Dewey also understood that it was difficult for arithmetic to make sense to the child if it was not applied to their lives. So, students used their math skills to build a tree house. After they read about the lives of Native American peoples on the prairie, they designed a tipi. They even used wool to make yarn and then make clothing from the yarn.

But it was also important for Dewey that the child found the answer for herself. Teachers at the Laboratory School were encouraged to help guide or facilitate student learning and not inundate their students with information. So, if a student was unsure of the answer, the teacher would help the student find the answer rather than give the student the answer. Dewey's Laboratory School was truly revolutionary and was noticed around the world.

It was also important to Dewey that the curriculum represent and present with a certain degree of symmetry, all the intrinsic factors in the human experience.[78] This was a curriculum that was democratic, socially efficient, and considered the needs of both school and society.[79]

Supporters of vocational education would also advocate reform in the curriculum, because they believed that schools were not preparing students for work-life after schooling. The educational historian Herbert Kliebard notes that "vocational education also fits perfectly into the social efficiency ideal of education as preparation for specific social and occupational role."[80] Advocates of vocational education insisted on a shift from apprenticeship to schooling, on the basis of training the new future workers and specialists in America. The thrust of this was at the heart of an educational debate that continued up until the turn of the twentieth century, culminating in the Smith-Hughes legislation, which established programs of federal assistance for teaching agricultural science, various trades, and home economics in high school.[81] Most of these programs would eventually benefit students interested in entering the industrial and technical workforce. I tell my students, next time if a plumber, carpenter, or electrician comes to your house ask them how they came to do what they do. Often, they will tell you that they felt school was a waste of time for them and that they wished they were exposed to their trade in school. Many schools in the United States were focused on the technical fields and offered courses in woodshop, drafting, sewing, home economics, and autobody.

In Gary, Indiana, William Wirt, the first superintendent of the Gary Schools adopted Dewey's model. Wirt who was a student of Dewey's came up with a long-term plan to reform Gary's Public Schools called the *Gary Plan.* The Gary Plan was also called the Work-Study-Play-Plan, which applied what students learned in the classroom to a rapidly growing industrial and manufacturing fields.[82] Like Dewey, Writ believed in a community of learn-ers as well as the notion that more could be produced if people knew how to work together, an approach that was incorporated in Gary's manufacturing and production industries.[83]

Wirt also came up with a revolutionary organizational structure that he called the "platoon system." In this system, students were divided into pla-toons based on where students were academically strongest.[84] There was as platoon for humanities, a platoon for the arts, a platoon for math and science, and a platoon for the industrial arts. Each platoon would learn from the other platoon. Wirt ultimately saw schooling as a playground, garden, workshop, social gathering, library, and academic classroom setting, where there were multiple ways to learn, but also to work in teams to help enhance the learning experience for every child.

Wirt's plan broke from what many saw as a highly bureaucratic and inef-ficient public school system. Gary Public Schools who served mostly children from working-class families became widely known as a hub for progressive education. Because of the training that students received at the Gary schools, many companies actively recruited Gary students for the practical training they received.

But there was resistance to Dewey's ideas as well as Writ's school plan. Many found that what students were learning drifted too far from a traditional education in the liberal arts and humanities and that public schools shouldn't train students for an industrial workforce. Dewey, however, argued that it was not about what students studied, but whether students were learning. Moreover, for Dewey, students learned just as much about carpentry as they did from traditional subjects such as history, math, or science.

By the turn of the twentieth century, psychologists and philosophers became increasingly interested in the field of education. Moreover, fields like developmental and social psychology would help impact the way teach-ers taught. The British mathematician and philosopher Alfred Whitehead (1861–1947), advocated against teaching what he called "inert ideas" which were ideas with no real application to the real world. Whitehead wrote, "In training a child to activity of though, above all things we must beware of what I will call 'inert ideas,' ideas that are merely received into the mind without being utilized, or tested, or thrown into fresh combinations."[85]

Like Whitehead, the American psychologist John B. Watson (1878–1958) believed that learning occurred purely through processes of association and reinforcement and that a child-centered approach to learning was the best teaching approach in schools.[86] Because of this new perspective of how children learned, a movement on school reform began to take shape. G. Stanley Hall (1846–1924), for example, argued that most public schools did not encourage learning but only stifled learning.[87] He suggested that schools create individual instruction for each child and tailor the curriculum around the developmental stages of children.[88] His plan was ambitious and did not consider the social and economic realities in schools and society.

Edward L. Thorndike (1874–1949) disagreed with Stanley's child-centered reforms. Thorndike, on the other hand, advocated for what he called *Social Engineering Reform*.[89] He believed that human nature could be altered, and schools and teachers could shape children in positive ways. Thorndike took away the individual experience of children in the classroom.[90] Such ideas were controversial even for their time. Not knowing the result of what were largely theoretical ideas on teaching and learning were challenged by teachers and school administrators who worked directly with students, but who also understood the realities of the school and classroom.

By the early 1900s, secondary school enrollments were increasing, but many questioned the type of education that students were receiving in public high schools. The educational historian William Reese writes:

> By World War I, a consensus emerged among leading educators that high school could be both efficient and democratic. That is, schools should open their doors as widely as possible but also offer a more practical curriculum to address the diverse needs and abilities of pupils.[91]

The National Education Association created a committee called the Commission on the Reorganization of Secondary Schools to address ways to reorganize secondary schools. In 1918, in a report titled *The Cardinal Principles of Secondary Education*, the Commission recommended that the secondary school curriculum be less academic and focus more on preparing students for work and life after high school.[92]

Progressivism no doubt changed the way that American society thought about the role of schools in society as well as the way that children learned in school, but such reforms also impacted teachers. Teacher jobs were being threatened because teachers were seen as being unwilling to adopt these new changes.

As early as 1897, teachers began working to organize and unionize. During this same year, the Chicago Teachers Federation (CTF) was established. CTF would eventually evolve into the Chicago Teachers Union (CTU). CTF was led for more than forty years by the charismatic and no-nonsense activist and reformer named Margaret Haley (1861–1939).

Today, Margaret Haley is considered the patron saint of America's teachers' unions. When CPS teachers went on strike in 2012, Karen Lewis the then president for the CTU took on city officials and major corporation the same way Margaret Haley did over 100 years before her, by exposing politicians for their backdoor deals in exempting private companies from paying taxes, monies that would go to the students and teachers. Margaret Haley biographer Kate Rousmaniere writes:

> Margaret Haley's life goal was to educate American citizens about the political economy of schooling. She did this through popular campaigns in which she instructed the public schools in school finance while exposing corporate tax deductions that drained school budgets, arguing that such practices not only undercut the quality of education of a majority of the nation's children but also perverted democracy.[93]

Margaret Haley was born in 1861 in Joliet, Illinois, some 45 miles southwest of Chicago. Her mother was an immigrant from Dublin, Ireland, while her father was born to Irish immigrants in Quebec, Canada. She was raised Catholic, but her parents were active members in several labor organizations and described themselves as agrarian activists.[94]

After attending the Illinois Normal School in Bloomington, Illinois, she moved to Chicago to teach sixth-grade students at the Hendricks School in the Stockyards District on the South Side of Chicago. The Stockyard District which is the setting of Upton Sinclair's famous novel *The Jungle* was inhabited mostly by European immigrants who worked the slaughterhouses for Chicago's bustling meat-packing industry. It was one of the poorest and most neglected neighborhoods in the city, where immigrants worked long hours for next to nothing. The children of these immigrants were rarely attended by their families. Haley found that the schools were also in poor condition and teachers lacked basic resources to help their students succeed. Many scholars argue that it was here that Haley's teacher activism was shaped.[95] Haley understood if the change was to come, teachers needed to organize and fight for their rights.

In 1897, Haley joined the CTF. By 1898, she became one of the organization's first district vice presidents. The organization members were mostly women and its membership was growing rapidly when Haley was appointed into her position.

A major concern for Haley was that teachers were earning less than unskilled factory workers and putting just as many hours as these workers did. Haley fought long and hard for most of her tenure as CTF president for higher teacher salaries, a secure pension system, job security through tenure, and better school conditions. She opposed William Rainey Harper's proposal to restructure CPSs to operate much like corporations, where school boards would be eliminated, and district superintendents would have more power to hire and fire teachers and principals. Haley also worried that Harper's model would only make schools like factories and corporations where schools would no longer prepare children for a free and democratic society but to help the rich become even wealthier.

Haley believed the soul of every school were its teachers, and children could not be successful if their teachers were given the resources to succeed. She was criticized for this even by the activist and social reformer Jane Addams, who felt that Haley cared more about teachers than the children in schools.

In 1901, Haley became president of the CTF and in 1904 as president of CTF she presented her famous address "Why Teachers Should Organize" to the National Association of Education (NEA) Convention. In her address to educators from around the country, she said:

> If the American people cannot be made to realize and meet their responsibility to the public school, no self-appointed custodians of the public intelligence and conscience can do it for them. . . . The methods as well as the objects of teachers' organizations must be in harmony with the fundamental object of the public school in a democracy, to preserve and develop the democratic ideal. It is not enough that this ideal be realized in the administration of the school and the methods of teaching; in all its relations to the public, the public school must conform to this ideal. Nowhere in the United States today does the public school, as a branch of the public service, receive from the public either the moral or financial support needed to enable it properly to perform its important function in the social organism.[96]

Her speech was an attack on the NEA for its lack of consideration to teachers and students in urban schools. Haley was called a "Bolshevik" and a "fiend in petticoats."[97] But she fought back. At the NEA's convention in Boston, she criticized the organization for not including women speakers among the hundreds scheduled to present at the convention.

Many agreed with her, and Haley was able to unite other organizations around her causes. Haley fought tirelessly for teachers and for students. Union leaders that came after her followed her lead. The American Teachers Federation (AFT) was founded in 1912. The issue of equal pay continued to be a major issue for teachers. In New York City, Grace S. Strachan took the issue of equal pay to the state capital. While teachers were organizing, and gaining influence, they lacked one major bargaining chip, their members who were mostly women could not yet vote. This would become a game changer in the fight for equal pay once women gained the right to vote in 1920, but it did not come without a fight.

## BROWN V. BOARD OF EDUCATION

Slavery is America's original sin. Much of America was built on the backs of enslaved people, forced here against their will to be under the complete control of their slave owners. There is a photo I show to my student of a young President Lydon Johnson standing behind a group of students (and some of their parents) outside a school. It is Johnson when he was a teacher/ principal in El Paso, Texas. Johnson is our first truly teacher president.

As a teacher, Johnson knew of the educational gaps in American schools and how schooling benefited whites. Most of his students were the children of migrant workers that knew that an education for their children was a way to achieve the American dream.

But educational gaps continue to plague American schools today. I teach my students about the landmark Supreme Court case *Brown v. Board of Education* and how President Johnson enforced the decision almost a decade later by threatening to cut federal funding to schools. In some ways, I do not like to teach it because I wonder how much has really changed.

History is presented as if everything was solved after *Brown v. Board of Education* and Johnson's enforcement of the law. But has it? America's past, good or bad, is often played out in our schools because schools are supposed to be bastions of American democracy. But are they? Have they always been this way?

During Reconstruction, the Port Royal Experiment offered a glimpse of what was possible for formerly enslaved people, it gave them land

**Figure 4.3 Lyndon B. Johnson with Students.** *Source:* Courtesy of LBJ Presidential Library.

and schools to learn.[98] But the majority of American schools in the South remained separate institutions, schools for whites and schools for blacks. The Jim Crow laws were a racists policy backed by law that created separate institutions for blacks and whites. It was the Northerners' way to help rebuilt and unite the country again and it was the white Souths (the losers of the Civil War) way to continue some semblance of their previous life.

Schools were also a favorite target for white supremacists—Frederick Douglass quibbled, "Schoolhouses are burnt, teachers mobbed and murdered, schools broken up."[99] Various court rulings reflected American racism and values when they made it legal for counties to spend more per student in white schools than for black schools. Black teachers were also discouraged because they were paid less and often had longer commutes to their schools. Skin color was the main obstacle to obtaining a proper education in the United States and not citizenship or human dignity.

Through various channels, intellectuals and activists such as Booker T. Washington and W. E. B. Du Bois led the way toward creating better and more equitable systems for black students. One of their lasting legacies was the creation of what are now known as Historically Black Colleges and Universities, many funded by whites to keep blacks out of white universities.

But racism and funding gaps persisted throughout the end of the nineteenth century and twentieth century. Despite the Supreme Court's decision in *Brown v. Board of Education* to desegregate American schools, local communities kept finding ways to separate white and black students based on location, financial means, and other factors.

Today, American students are still largely segregated by skin color, and this is particularly evident in the city of Chicago. According to a WBEZ article from 2019, white families "have kind of a history of sending their kids to private schools or parochial schools," according to Devon Herrick, principal of Hancock College Prep. The city's twelve selective enrollment high schools, which students have to test into, look at socioeconomic status, but not race, as a factor for admittance. This leads to marginal diversity at these schools and a strong sense of segregation at traditional neighborhood schools, which reflects Chicago's racially segregated neighborhoods.

## DECADE AFTER DECADE OF REFORMS

Today, it is almost impossible to take politics out of education. Educational reforms have been contentious, and political. Often, they are referred to in terms of traditional versus progressive. Arguably, traditionalists believe that schools should maintain the status quo or go back to the way things were, while progressives argue that schools should adapt to the needs of a changing society and change according to those needs.

Politically one could put traditionalists in the category of conservatives and progressives in the category of liberals, but neither would fit perfectly in either category. A drastic change too far to the left or too far to the right would be considered radical. Teachers sometimes get in the middle of many of these reforms. Some see them as recycled ideas that are only reprocessed or repurposed, with nothing new being offered. Others welcome the reforms as a way to solve some of the problems in schools.

In the 1950s, many Americans worried that the Soviet Union would surpass the United States. Teachers became criticized for not preparing students to compete against the Soviets. Albert Lynd's famous book *Quackery in the Public Schools* attacked teachers for what he called "mediocre academic standards" and "poor teacher quality."[100] The successful launch of Sputnik by the Soviet Union in 1957 only added to American's worries.

In 1958, the National Education Act was passed, and federal funding was provided to public schools to help raise academic standards. Students found that there were more courses in math and science as well as in foreign languages. Teacher training programs raised their admission standards and new courses were introduced to help train teachers to teach in these new subjects.

By the mid-1960s, political and social movements sought to revise the school curriculum. The school curriculum was expanded to include the voices of marginalized groups such as African Americans, Native Americans, Latinos, and women. In many universities, the core curriculum required students to take courses on non-Western subjects. Those that defended the changes found them to reflect the cultural pluralism of the time, something that was long overdue. Those that opposed the changes worried about the long-term impact these changes would have on American culture and values.

How does one decide what to include or leave out in the school curriculum? Or what American values, if any, should be taught in schools? Questions like these became highly contentious to the point that they became part of *Culture Wars* in the United States.

My favorite case occurred in Texas. Some in Texas felt that Texas school textbooks did not do enough to reflect America's Christian legacy. Some wanted the textbooks to say that Christianity and Christian values led the forefathers to seek independence and create American democracy. Furthermore, they wanted the textbooks to say that the greatest legal documents in the United States such as the *U.S Constitution* and *Declaration of Independence* were inspired by a Christian worldview. While many of the forefathers were raised Christian, it is uncertain how important Christianity was in their lives. We know that some were religious while others were not. Key figures like Thomas Jefferson, John Adams, and Ethan Allen were Deists and Unitarians, which neglected the Trinity, a core belief in Christianity. Rather than saying just this, the Texas school textbooks were painting a picture that made the forefathers look as if they were religious zealots, and that Christianity was the driving force behind their inspiration for the founding of America.

In another equally interesting case, Martin Bernal's publication of *Black Athena* in 1987 argued that the ancient Greeks had been largely influenced by the ancient Egyptians and Phoenicians and that many of the ideas that originated from ancient Greece, actually came from Africa.[101] Afro-centrists wanted school textbooks to be revised to reflect this. Most historians today would agree that the ancient Greeks borrowed from the Egyptians, Phoenicians, and elsewhere, but that the ancient Greeks were never heavily influenced by none. And what they did borrow that made to be uniquely Greek.

The influence on the ancient Greeks was taken a step further when some argued that the ancient Egyptians borrowed from sub-Saharan African culture and civilization and thus the ancient Greeks, who were influenced by the ancient Egyptians, proved that Western civilization originated in Africa. There was even a case of a history professor named Dr. Leonard Jeffries from City College of New York, who taught his students that Plato had studied at the Library of Alexandria, in Egypt, and it was there that Western philosophy originated. Jeffries's teachings were problematic, but what Jeffries ignored was that the Library of Alexandria would not be built until almost three generations after Plato.

This, like the case in Texas was a misrepresentation of history and the facts. But this goes back to my original question: Who decides what is taught in schools and how it is taught? Today we see statues of confederate generals and other confederate symbols being taken down. We also see parents getting into these physical confrontations with other parents about critical race theory. For some, it is much to do about nothing but for others, it means the end of America as we know it.

It is true that many Americans feel connected to America's past and to the people that help make up that past. Many people may be very well related to some of those historical figures we learn about in school. I am sure we all have had an ancestor somewhere in our *genos* who did great things, but it is also probably just as likely that we have had an ancestor who has done some horrible things. We have to remember that is not us, but that was them. I had someone once say to me, "How would you like if they talked crap about your great, great, great grandfather." I told them, "I didn't know my great, great, great grandfather, so I guess I wouldn't care." Teaching our students what happened is important, but only if we teach them what really happened. Both the good and the bad. That is how our students learn to continue doing what is good and keeping the bad from happening again.

The 1970s and 1980s once again demanded higher academic standards and more accountability on teachers as well as reforming school finances. The 1983 report *A Nation at Risk* called for states to raise their graduation requirements and offer more courses in the sciences, mathematics, and foreign languages. Part of the report said:

> If an unfriendly foreign power had attempted to impose on America the mediocre educational performance that exists today, we might well have viewed it as an act of war. As it stands, we have allowed this to happen to ourselves. We have even squandered the gains in student achievement made in the wake of the Sputnik challenge. Moreover, we have dismantled essential support systems which helped make those gains possible. We have, in effect, been committing an act of unthinking, unilateral educational disarmament.

The report framed this dire need to reform in terms of Cold War language, that if something was not done soon, the Soviets and their allies would surpass the United States. in almost every possible way. But the United States never ranked first in any international exams, not then and not today. The assumption is that because a nation does well on international exams, they will surpass other nations socially, politically, economically, and militarily. But that has not been the case if we look last sixty years. The U.S. students have never come first on PISA or TIMMS, two major international exams, but American students are still coming up with the most creative and innovative ideas in the world. So, something is being done right by teachers and schools. Just look at the most successful companies in the world in the last fifty years, almost all created by Americans who were trained in American schools.

In higher education, the United States is still the number one destination for foreign students. The U.S. colleges and universities as a whole rank higher than in any other country in the world. In 2014, there was a record number, 820,000 foreign students who entered American colleges and universities.[102] The biggest chunk came from China, with 235,000 students. It is estimated that this brought in 24 billion dollars to the U.S. economy. American education is a hot commodity. To have a degree from an American university opens doors that would not be possible elsewhere. An overwhelming number of these foreign students are studying, engineering, computer science, and business. At one point China worried that their students would not return back to China, that the Chinese government offered American universities to build them a campus in China.

What the *Nation a Risk* was really trying to do was to instill fear in the public so politicians could get the support they needed to implement changes to American schools. Not surprisingly, it worked. The reforms would continue well into the second decade of the 2000s regardless of who was president. It would become a major priority for those running in politics, and it would be difficult for anyone to get elected if they did not have a long-term plan for education.

By the 1990s, teacher accountability and raising standards in schools continued. Merit pay was introduced in some schools and the expansion of charter schools continued in many major American cities. Equity and excellence were an overarching theme for many of the reforms, giving every child their fair shot to a good education and that every child in America deserved a challenging curriculum that would prepare them for the twenty-first century. For many, the reforms were well-intentioned but others questioned if they were truly realistic and if they understood the real concerns and struggles of most communities in America.

When Bill Clinton became president in 1992 his administration sought to take the American student to the next century by expanding educational opportunity. College attendance and graduation rates were increased after low-interest loans were provided to students. The key features of the Clinton-Gore administration on education were as follows:

- Implementing standards in core subjects and increasing high school graduation.
- Targeting Title I funds to high-poverty schools and requiring States and school districts to turn around low-performing schools.
- Expand public school choice and supporting the growth of public charter schools.
- Providing $1.2 billion for urgent school renovation as well as a repair fund to Native American schools.[103]

By the 2000s, reforms included increasing high school graduation requirements, mandating state-wise testing programs, offering more Advancement Placement and International Baccalaureate courses, welcoming the use of technology in the classroom and introducing new ways in evaluating teachers.

Leave No Child Behind was first proposed in the 1990s but would later find momentum as No Child Left Behind during the George W. Bush presidency. The achievement gap in schools nationwide was growing and Latino and African American students continued to lag behind white students. No Child Left Behind was presented as focusing on the schools and not on the individual teacher and student. But teachers and students would feel the brunt of this new measure. Schools that failed to meet proficiency in the core subjects were declared as "failing." Schools were also forced to compete with one another for federal funds, and school districts that did to meet performance goals did not receive federal funding. For many, the idea of rewarding schools did not make sense because it was the schools that were not performing that needed the most help.

The leading education initiative during the Obama administration was Race to the Top or Reforming Education Through Race to the Top. Race to the Top had several goals and like all educational initiatives before it was controversial. Race to the Top was sought to:

- Provide $4 billion on a competitive basis to states that developed rigorous standards and better assessments.
- New data systems to provide information about student progress.
- Support for teachers and school leaders to become more effective.
- Increased emphasis and resources for the rigorous interventions needed to turn around the lowest-performing schools.[104]

Through Race to the Top, states were challenged to submit applications that proposed ways to improving schools. Applications were competitive and states that focused on STEM education were prioritized. In total, forty-six states and the District of Columbia submitted comprehensive reform plans. Of these applicants, nineteen received state funding, thirty-four states modified state education laws or policies to facilitate needed change, and forty-eight states worked together to create a voluntary set of rigorous college- and career-ready standards.

## NOTES

1. Warren, Donald, ed. (1989). *American Teachers: Histories of a Profession at Work*. New York: Macmillan Publishing Company, p. 23.

2. Ibid.

3. Cott, Nancy F. (1997). *The Bonds of Womanhood: Women's Sphere in England, 1780-1835*. New Haven, CT: Yale University Press.

4. Ibid.

5. *Rules for Teachers*. (1915). Old Sacramento Schoolhouse Museum. http://oldsacschoolhouse.scoe.net/visit/index.html Retrieved October 5, 2018.

6. In Barnard, Henry, ed. (1861). *Memoirs of Educators*. New York: F.C. Brownell, p. 135.

7. Lord, J. (1873). *The Life of Emma Willard*. New York: D. Appleton and Co.

8. Fairbanks, Mary Mason. (1898). *Emma Willard and Her Pupils or Fifty Years of Troy Female Seminary, 1822-1872*. New York: Mrs. Russell Sage Publications.

9. Ibid.

10. Repousis, Angelo. (2004). "The Trojan Women: Emma Hart Willard and the Troy Society for the Advancement of Female Education in Greece." *Journal of the Early Republic*, 24(3), pp. 445–476.

11. Goodsell, Willystine. (1970). *Pioneers of women's education in the United States: Emma Willard, Catherine Beecher, Mary Lyon*. New York: AMS Press.

12. Beecher, Catharine. (1846). *The Evils Suffered by American Women and American Children: The Causes and the Remedy / Presented in an Address by C.E. Beecher, to Meetings of Ladies in Cincinnati, Washington, Baltimore, Philadelphia, New York, and Other Cities. Also, An Address to the Protestant Clergy of the United States.* New York: Harper & Brothers, p. 3.

13. Vinovskis, Maris A. and Bernard, Richard M. (1978). "Beyond Catharine Beecher: Female Education in the Antebellum Period." *Signs.* 3(4), pp. 856–869.

14. Burstyn, Joan N. (1974). "Catharine Beecher and the Education of American Women." *The New England Quarterly,* 47(3), pp. 386–403.

15. Turpin, Andrea L. (2010). "The Ideological Origins of the Women's College: Religion, Class and Curriculum in the Educational Visions of Catharine Beecher and Mary Lyon." *History of Education Quarterly,* 50(2), pp. 133–158.

16. Barry, Kathleen. (2000). *Susan B. Anthony: A Biography of a Singular Feminist.* 1st Book Library.

17. Ibid.

18. Perkins, Linda M. (1983). "The Impact of the Cult of True Woman Hood on Black Women." *Journal of Social Issues,* 39(3), pp. 17–28.

19. Mabee, Carleton. (1968). "A Negro Boycott to Integrate Boston Schools." *New England Quarterly,* 41(3), pp. 341–361.

20. Cimbala, Paul A. and Miller, Randal M., ed. (1999). *The Freedmen's Bureau and Reconstruction: Reconsiderations.* New York: Fordham University Press.

21. See Du Bois, W.E.B. (2002). *The Education of Black People: Ten Critiques, 1906-1960.* Monthly Review Press.

22. Du Bois, W.E.B. (1901). *The Negro Common School.* Atlanta, GA: University Press.

23. Department of Education. (1870). *Report of the Commissioner of Education on the Improvement of Public Schools in the District of Columbia.* Washington, DC: Government Printing Office.

24. U.S. Census Bureau. (1918). *Negro Population in the United States, 1790-1915.* Washington, DC: Government Printing.

25. Butchart, Ronald E. (2010). *Schooling and the Freed People: Teaching, Learning, and the Struggle for Black Freedom, 1861-1876.* Chapel Hill, NC: University of North Carolina Press.

26. Douty, Esther Morris. (1971). *Charlotte Forten, Free Black Teacher.* Garrard Publishing Co.

27. Emmanuel, Nelson S. ed. (2000). *African American Authors, 1745-1945: A Biographical and Critical Sourcebook.* Westport, CT and London: Greenwood Press.

28. Ibid.

29. Forten, Charlotte. (1981). *The Journal of Charlotte L. Forten: A Free Negro in the Slave Era.* New York: W.W. Norton & Company, p. 132.

30. See Pollizer, William S. (1999). *The Gullah People and Their African Heritage.* Athens, GA: University of Georgia Press.

31. Ibid.

32. Forten, Charlotte. (1864). "Life on the Sea Islands." *Atlantic Monthly*. https://www.theatlantic.com/magazine/archive/1864/05/life-on-the-sea-islands/308758/ Retrieved October 30, 2018.

33. Taylor, Kay Ann. (2005). "Mary S. Peake and Charlotte L. Forten: Black Teachers During the Civil War Reconstruction." *The Journal of Negro Education*, 74(2), pp. 124–137.

34. Harrison, Robert. (2011). *Washington During Civil War and Reconstruction: Race and Radicalism*. Cambridge and New York: Cambridge University Press.

35. May, Vivian M. (2012). *Anna Julia Cooper, Visionary Black Feminist: A Critical Introduction*. New York and London: Routledge.

36. May, Vivian M. (2015). *Anna Julia Cooper, Visionary Black Feminist: A Critical Introduction*. London, UK: Routledge.

37. Coppin, Fanny. (1913). *Reminiscences of School Life, and Hints on Teaching*. Philadelphia, PA: African Methodist Episcopal Book Concern.

38. Ibid.

39. Gates, Henry Louis and Higginbotham, Evelyn Brooks. ed. (2004). *African American Lives*. London and New York. Oxford University Press.

40. Perkins, Linda Marie. (1978). *Fanny Jackson Coppin and the Institute for Colored Youth: A Model of Nineteenth Century Black Female Educational and Community Leadership, 1837-1902*. Unpublished Dissertation. University of Illinois at Urbana-Champaign.

41. Smith, Eric Ledell. (2003). "To Teach My People: Fanny Jackson Coppin and Philadelphia's Institute for Colored Youth." *Pennsylvania Heritage*, 29(1), pp. 6–11.

42. Perkins, Linda Marie. (1978). *Fanny Jackson Coppin and the Institute for Colored Youth: A Model of Nineteenth Century Black Female Educational and Community Leadership, 1837-1902*. Unpublished Dissertation. University of Illinois at Urbana-Champaign.

43. Turner, Frederick Jackson (2016). *The Frontier in American History*. Palala Press.

44. Fowler, William Worthington. (2015). *Woman on the American Frontier: A Valuable and Authentic History of the Heroism, Adventures, Privations, Captivities, Trials, and Noble Lives and Deaths of the Pioneer Mothers of the Republic*. Repressed Publishing.

45. Beecher, Catherine. (2016). *The Duty of American Women to Their Country*. Palala Press.

46. Steinbeck, John. (2003). *East of Eden*. Viking Press, p. 146.

47. Snyder, Thomas D., ed. (1993). *120 Years of American Education: A Statistical Portrait*. Washington, DC: National Center of Educational Statistics.

48. Ibid.

49. Ibid.

50. Adams, Wallace David. (1995). *Education for Extinction: American Indians and the Boarding School Experience, 1875-1928*. Missouri, KS: University of Kansas Press.

51. Graber, Kay ed. (2004). *Sister to the Sioux: The Memoirs of Elaine Goodale Eastman 1885-1891*. Lincoln, NE: University of Nebraska Press, p. 73.

52. Diamond, Jared. (2017). *Guns, Germs, and Steel: The Fates of Human Societies*. W.W. Norton & Company, p. 195.

53. Shaw, Ann Marie. (1903). "The True Character of New York Public Schools." *World Works*, 7(2), p. 4206.

54. Zervas, Theodore G. (2017). "Finding a Balance in Education: Immigration, Diversity, and Schooling in Urban America, 1890-1900." *Athens Journal of Education*, 4(1), pp. 77–84.

55. Ibid.

56. Fass, Paula S. (1989). *Outside In: Minorities and the Transformation of American Education*. London and New York: Oxford University Press, p. 16.

57. Snyder, Thomas D. ed. (1993). *120 Years of American Education: A Statistical Portrait*. Washington, DC: National Center of Educational Statistics.

58. Ibid.

59. Gillam, Victor, F. (1890). "The Inevitable Result to the American Workingman of Unrestricted Immigration." Chromolithograph. *Judge*.

60. William Seward, Annual Message to the Legislature (1840) *reprinted in* BAKER, *supra* note 168, pp. 212–213.

61. Burns, J.A. (1910). *The Growth and Development of the Catholic School System in the United States*. New York and Cincinnati: Benzinger Brothers, p. 216.

62. Ibid.

63. Antin, May. (1912). *The Promised Land*. Boston, MA and New York: Hougton Mifflin Company.

64. Bodnar, John. (1987). *The Transplanted: A History of Immigrants in Urban America*. Bloomington, IN: Indiana University Press, p. 190.

65. Saloutos, Theodore. (1956). *They Remember America: The Story of Repatriated Greek Americans*. Los Angeles, CA: University of California Press, p. 22.

66. Zervas, Theodore G. and Papadopoulos, Alex. (2019). "Creating Greeks and Greek-Americans: Geographic and Educational Identity Constructions at the *Socrates* and *Koraes* Greek-American Schools." *European Education*, 52(1), pp. 1–21.

67. Soumakis, Fevronia and Zervas, Theodore G. ed. (2020). *Educating Greek Americans: Historical and Contemporary Pathways*. New York and London: Palgrave & Macmillan.

68. Ibid.

69. Renner, Marguerite. (1981). *Who Will Teach? Changing Job Opportunity and Roles for Women in the Evolution of the Pittsburgh Public Schools, 1830-1900*. Unpublished Dissertation. University of Pittsburgh.

70. Ibid.

71. Ibid.

72. Gradel, Thomas J., Simpson, Dick, and Zenellis, Andris. (2008). "Curing Corruption in Illinois: Anti-Corruption Report Number 1." Unpublished. University of Illinois at Chicago Department of Political Science. p. 1.

73. Ibid.

74. Berrol, Selma Contor. (1993). *Julia Richman: A Nobel Woman*. Philadelphia, PA: Balch Institute for Ethnic Studies.

75. Ibid.

76. Richman, Julia. (1905). "The Immigrant Child." In *Journal of Proceedings and Addresses of the Forty-Fourth Annual Meeting*. Winona, MN: National Educational Association, p. 113.

77. Dewey, John. (1938). *John Dewey Experience and Education*. New York: Simon & Shuster.

78. Kliebard, Herbert M. (1986). *The Struggle for the American Curriculum: 1893-1958*. Routledge & Kegan Paul.

79. Dewey, John. (1916). *Democracy and Education*. New York: The Free Press.

80. Ibid, p. 151.

81. Tyack, David. (1995). *Tinkering toward Utopia: A Century of Public School Reform*. Harvard University Press.

82. Thorburn, Michael. (2017). "John Dewey, William Wirt and the Gary Schools Plan: A Centennial Reappraisal." *Journal of Educational Administration and History*, 2(49), pp. 144–156.

83. Ibid.

84. Kaluf, Kevin, J. and Rogers, George E. (2011). "The Gary Plan: A Model for Today's Education?" *Journal of STWM Teacher Education*, 48(1).

85. Whitehead, Alfred North. (1929). *The Aims of Education and Other Essays*. New York: The Free Press, p. 1.

86. Watson, John B. (1924). *Behaviorism*. New York: W.W. Norton & Company.

87. Stanley, G. Hall. (1906). *Youth its Education, Regimen, and Hygiene*. New York: D. Appleton and Company.

88. Ibid.

89. Thorndike, Edward Lee. (1904). *An Introduction to the Theory of Mental and Social Measurements*. New York: The Science Press.

90. Thorndike, Edward Lee. (1906). *The Principles of Teaching Based on Psychology*. Syracuse, NY: The Mason-Henry Press.

91. Reese, William J. (2005). *America's Public Schools: From the Common School to "No Child Left Behind."* Baltimore, MD: John Hopkins University Press, p. 189.

92. National Education Association of the United States. (1918). *Cardinal Principles of Secondary Education. A Report of the Commission on the Reorganization of Secondary Education appointed by the National Education Association*. Bulletin No. 5.

93. Rousmaniere, Kate. (2005). *Citizen Teacher: The Life and Leadership of Margaret Haley*. Albany, NY: State University New York Press, p. ix.

94. Reid, Robert L. (1982). *Battleground the Autobiography of Margaret Haley*. Chicago, IL: University of Illinois Press.

95. Ibid.

96. Haley, Margaret. (1904). "Why Teachers Should Organize." *Journal of Education*, 60(18).

97. Tyack, David and Hansot, Elizabeth. (1992). *Learning Together: A History of Coeducation in American Public Schools*. New York: Russell Sage Foundation.

98. Rose, Willie Lee Nichols (1999). *Rehearsal for Reconstruction the Port Royal Experiment.* Athens, GA: University of Georgia Press.

99. Douglas, Fredrick. (1852). "What to a Slave, is the Fourth of July."

100. Lynd, Albert. (1953). *Quackery in Public Schools.* New York: Little, Brown & Company.

101. Bernal, Martin. (1987). *Black Athena: The Afroasiatic Roots of Classical Civilization.* New Brunswick, NJ: Rutgers University Press.

102. Institute of International Education. U.S. Bureau of Educational and Cultural Affairs. http://www.iie.org/en/Research-and-Publications/Open-Doors/Data /International-Students Retrieved Jan 7, 2014.

103. See *The Clinton and Gore: A Record of Progress.* (1999). https://clinton-whitehouse5.archives.gov/WH/Accomplishments/eightyears-05.html Retrieved Oct 1, 2021.

104. See *Race to the Top: Education Knowledge and the Skills for the Jobs for the Future.* https://obamawhitehouse.archives.gov/issues/education/k-12/race-to-the-top *Retrieved Nov 18, 2021.*

# Chapter 5

# Democracy and Education

Today, Chicago Public Schools (CPSs) is the third-largest school district in the United States. New York City Public Schools is the largest with 1,700 schools, over 1 million students, and 75,000 teachers. Los Angeles Public Schools, the second-largest school district in America, has 670,000 students, 27,000 teachers, and 1,300 schools. CPS operates 633 schools and enrolls over 377,000 students and nearly 19,000 teachers. Over 39,000 people work for CPSs and the district is the second-largest employer in the city of Chicago. I began my teaching career in CPS and many of my pre-service teachers go on to teach in CPSs.

While CPS is the largest school district in Chicago and Illinois, the charter school system in Chicago is also robust. Today there are 126 charter schools in Chicago with more than 57,000 students enrolled in a charter school across the city. The Archdiocese of Chicago which covers the city of Chicago and nearby Chicago suburbs operates 209 schools with more than 62,000 students enrolled in an Archdiocese school.

The school system in Chicago is no different from many of the other school systems found in cities across America. They are not easy to manage and are entrenched within the politics of their city. CPS is no exception to this. It is administered through Central Office, and the head of schools or CEO makes school-wide decisions across the district. The school board and the teacher's union seem to have always been at odds with one another over issues of equity, teacher's pay, school performance, school facilities, and the best way to educate students.

No school in Chicago is the same. You could drive a mile from one school to another and find that two schools are not alike. But a one-size-fits-all model has been applied to most schools in CPS. This has been an ongoing issue and raises the question of how to best support the schools in the district.

## SAVAGE INEQUALITIES

Each teacher builds their own systems for their classroom. From expectations and policies to objectives and assessments, teachers create a community of learners. Many teachers ask the question: "How can I make my classroom fair and equitable for all my students?"

Part of creating an equitable classroom is recognizing the stigmas and burdens with which students enter. Some students simply need more attention than others, both to combat stereotypes and to valorize their experiences. An equitable teacher welcomes the experiences of her students, first by recognizing the historical and political weight that her students carry into the classroom, and then by creating opportunities to help the entire class learn for one another. This is one of the reasons why a diverse classroom is important to the learning process. It is not only about bringing in ideas but allowing students to feel they can express themselves.

Policies as well as how we evaluate our students should be standardized enough to create an even landscape but flexible enough to accommodate diverse needs. Many teachers inspire a vision for a classroom that recognizes and compensates for the severe burdens that continue to oppress or stigmatize students' lives. The educational historian Joel Spring argues that "equality of opportunity is based on the idea of an *unequal* society where individuals compete with one another, with some becoming wealthy and some falling to the bottom of the economic scale."[1] Giving all students their fair shot to be able to move up the social ladder is what was envisioned for the first public schools in the United States. But not all students get their fair shot to succeed.

In 1991, Jonathan Kozol published his eye-opening book *Savage Inequalities*. I first read Kozol's book when I was preparing to become a teacher. I could say that not much has changed today since Kozol first published his book. Kozol visited schools across the country (East Saint Louis, Chicago, Washington, DC, Cincinnati, New York, and San Antonio). He writes about what he observed and the conversations he had with teachers, principals, administrators, and students about their schools. Kozol found schools that some had state-of-the-art equipment, multiple gymnasiums, college preparatory classes, up to date textbooks, clean and well-kept buildings, and adequate teacher-student ratios. He also found schools that were understaffed, crowded, and in physical decay.

The savage inequalities that Kozol writes about stem largely from a disparity in funding, which is in large part due to racial segregation. Homeowners in wealthier communities contribute more toward their schools because of their higher property taxes, giving these schools more resources, better-qualified teachers, and better facilities for their students. However, the school inequalities that Kozol writes about in his book resulted from economic disparity and concentrated disadvantage, precipitated through systematic racism. Historically, many whites viewed the dramatic increase of African American migrants near their communities with fear and hostility. Many white families fled to the suburbs because they did not want their children attending school with black children.

Many sociologists have found that housing segregation and the creation of black ghettos began with whites, through their neighborhood associations and realtors, taking up collections to buy out African American homeowners.[2] If that didn't work, neighborhood associations often implemented restrictive housing covenants that would not permit African Americans to rent or purchase property in the community. This is better known today as redlining or intentionally keeping black families out of white neighborhoods.

Whites were also able to create racial segregation by relocating and each white family had its own personal limit for their acceptability of "blackness" in their neighborhood. When the first black family moved in, the white family with the lowest limit moved out, leaving room for another black family to move in. The cycle repeated itself until the white neighborhood became a black one.[3] Home values today are tied to school performance. The better the school, the more likely a home's price will increase. Talk to any real estate agent and ask them if people buy homes and they will tell you that people don't buy homes but schools and communities for their children. The major real estate websites now offer a school score, usually 1 to 10, which can impact home prices.

Even today there is a significant disparity in the amount of funding going to schools in affluent neighborhoods versus poor neighborhoods. Detroit Public Schools spend just over 10,000 per student while the nearby suburb of Gross Pointe spends 14,000 more per student. In CPSs, the average expenditure per pupil is about 16,000, while Wilmette, Illinois, just north of Chicago, spends just over 19,000. Tie school expenditures to family income and education and, one will find that it is no wonder that more affluent schools produce better attendance records, higher standardized test scores, more national merit scholars, higher graduation rates, and higher college placement rates.

## LOSING ONE'S COOL

In Thomas Chatterton Williams's *Losing My Cool*, Williams writes about growing up biracial and struggling to find his racial identity. In middle school, he embraces the brash hip-hop culture of the 1990s, while eschewing anything that did not reflect the perceived tenets of the genre. Being *cool*, to Williams, meant that one solely espoused the misogynistic attitudes of the hip-hop stars he admired. It was not until college that Williams realizes that because of his struggle in finding who he was, he missed out on many other important experiences. Nonetheless, this awakening still allowed him to grow and to adopt a new meaning of *cool* for himself.

As Williams notes in his book, "Despite my mother's being white, we were a black and not an interracial family. Both my parents stressed this distinction and the result was that, growing up, race was not so complicated an issue in our household. My brother and I were black period." Identity plays a critical role in Williams's journey. He is trying to figure out how to navigate his world, be true to himself, and to be seen as "an authentic black man," by his peers. Even though he comes from a loving and nurturing middle-class family, he and his friends do not openly embrace those inherent values. After all, those values were deemed *uncool*. It's not until Williams enters college at Georgetown University that he begins to truly appreciate his father's love for books. *Love, Literature, and a Black Man's Escape from the Crowd* is the subtitle of Williams's books. It alludes to the complex nature of coming into one's own.

Race and identity are important in America. One only needs to look at American history. We are a race-conscious nation. Much more than other nations in the world. Williams's view of identity and race led him to embrace his "blackest" while denying essential aspects of himself. Trying to fit in and to be seen as *cool* has caused so many to act as if we were someone else, in order to be seen as *real*. I love Williams's book because it talks about those universal struggles of finding oneself.

## SEEKING QUALITY AND LIMITING INEQUALITY

I show this image (figure 5.1) to my students. I ask them how the image helps explain the difference between "equality" and "equity." The answer is very simple: equality means give everybody the same while equity means give people what they need. We can't assume that all our students will succeed if they are given the same resources the same way we would not expect a special education student to succeed if they were given the same textbook used by an honor student.

After I show the image to my class, I ask my students to think about how they plan to make their classrooms more equitable for all their students. While they discuss my question, I present to them figure 5.2. I then say to them, while we can give students the support they need to succeed, it shouldn't be our long-term goal to bring down any systematic barriers that keep kids from succeeding? It tries to get them to think about what those barriers are that many students face both in and outside school.

The difference of equity and equality has also become a popular teacher interview question. After an interview, I ask my students what were some

**Figure 5.1 Equity vs. Equality with Supports.** Equality vs. Equity—by the Interaction Institute for Social Change. *Source:* Artist: Angus Maguire. Image Found: interaction institute.org.

of the questions they were asked during their interview? I try to write them down so I don't forget them. Below are some of the questions my students were asked in a teaching interview these past few years.

1) What do you think it means to be conscious about culture and race in an educational environment?
2) How does your awareness race and culture impact your work with students, colleagues, and families? Please be specific.
3) How to organize your classroom/group to maximize the time available for learning?
4) What is your current thinking about equity, and how has your thinking changed over time? Specifically, how are you looking to grow in your practice of leading/teaching with a racial equity lens?
5) How do you assess student performance and progress? Provide an example of how you have used this data to inform your lesson planning and instruction.
6) Provide an example of how you have or would integrate technology into student learning experiences.
7) Describe the skills or attributes you believe are necessary to be an outstanding teacher.
8) How would you address a wide range of skills in your classroom?

## EQUALITY VERSUS EQUITY

In the first image, it is assumed that everyone will benefit from the same supports. They are being treated equally.

In the second image, individuals are given different supports to make it possible for them to have equal access to the game. They are being treated equitably.

In the third image, all three can see the game without any supports or accommodations because the cause of the inequity was addressed. The systemic barrier has been removed.

**Figure 5.2   Equity vs. Equality without Supports.** A picture illustrating the concepts of equality, equity, and justice. *Source:* Courtesy of Advancing Equity and Inclusion: A Guide for Municipalities, by City for All Women Initiative (CAWI), Ottawa.

9) Briefly discuss two or three components of effective classroom management.

10) What is your philosophy of education?

All are good questions, except maybe the last one.

## WHAT DOES ARCHDUKE FRANZ FERDINAND AND GEORGE FLOYD HAVE IN COMMON?

When I taught history to high school students, one of my favorite topics was World War I and the events that led up to the War. In 1914, Archduke Franz Ferdinand, heir apparent to the Austro-Hungarian throne, was visiting Sarajevo with his wife Sophie, Duchess of Hohenberg.

Sarajevo, the capital of Bosnia, had been under Ottoman control for over 300 years. The Ottoman Empire was gradually declining, and Bosnia was seeking to break away from its colonial ruler. Bosnia however was being courted by both Serbia and Austria-Hungary. Serbia felt that Bosnia should join them because of cultural and historical reasons but Austria-Hungary, a major European power, saw Bosnia as the next logical addition to its growing empire.

The fate of Bosnia became highly politicized as both Serbia and Austria-Hungary vied to take control of it. As soon as Bosnia looked like it was going to Austria-Hungary, nationalist groups in Serbia and Bosnia organized swearing that Bosnia would never be controlled by the Austro-Hungarian Empire. One of these groups was called the *Black Hand*, a ragtag ultra-nationalist group made up of a group of young nationalist zealots. The *Black Hand* planned to assassinate the Archduke and the Duchesses once they visited Sarajevo.

On June 25, 1914, the Duke and Duchesses arrived in Sarajevo. From all accounts, it was a warm sunny day. The royal couple planned to travel in the back of an open-air car through the streets of downtown Sarajevo while they waved and smiled at a cheering crowd.

The nationalist fervor in Bosnia was nothing seen before in Europe. People tended to feel an allegiance to their families or local communities, but by the late nineteenth century people saw themselves as being part of a broader nation united around a common language, religion, and history. Some people were willing to die for their nations. But let's go back a bit further.

By the nineteenth century, the balance of power in Europe had shifted. New nations such as Greece, Bulgaria, Serbia, Montenegro, and Romania emerge. A united Italy and Germany are created in the early 1870s, and the agreement made after the Napoleonic Wars (The Treaty of Vienna, 1815), to keep Europe's borders as they were, was no longer enforced. Things were changing quickly, and people were worried that a war was in the horizon.

When the Archduke and Duchess finally arrive in Sarajevo they get in the back of their car and begin to drive through the streets of the city. The *Black Hand* planned to assassinate them by throwing a bomb in their car. As they drive through downtown Sarajevo waving to passersby, a member of the *Black Hand* throws a bomb at their car but misses the car.

The Duke and Duchess are rattled but unscathed. Nobody else is hurt. The royal couple decide to continue their planned schedule and stop at a local hospital to visit the sick and dying and then continue their tour of the city. After they leave the hospital, Princip Gavrilo, an eighteen-year-old member of the *Black Hand* who had gone unnoticed during the bomb incident, was walking through the streets of Sarajevo when the Duke and Duchess's car happened to stop right in front of him. Gavrilo walked up to the car pulled out his pistol, shot the driver and then shot the Duke and Duchess. All three were killed.

When World War I started, most people assumed it was over the assassination of the Archduke and Duchess. But the fact is the murder of the Archduke and Duchess was merely the straw that broke the camel's back. Some 20 million people were killed fighting in World War I. More people were killed in that war than any other war before it.

When George Floyd was killed in Minneapolis on May 25, 2020, by a police officer, many believed that the protests that followed were about police brutality. But it was not just about that. Things had been brewing in America for sometime.

It's true, the black community in America had gotten tired of being accused of crimes they did not commit, and for being killed by the police for no reason. But the injustices caused on the community were much deeper than that.

The argument by those who opposed the Black Lives Matter movement was that it ignored black on black crime and only cared to attack the police, an institution that protected them from hurting themselves and hurting others. But that wasn't the case at all.

The movement was about all the injustices that have occurred to the black community in America. They were frustrated that black people were more likely to be killed by police than any other group, that black people were more likely to be poor, to die from a preventable disease, and to be jailed.

For decades a plethora of books, articles, and opinions were written and made available about the all injustices occurring to the African American community in the United States, to the point that the community was screaming for help, but nobody was listening. Until the last straw that broke the camel's back.

## GENDER IDENTITY, RACIAL IDENTITY, AND PRONOUNS

In an episode of the animated series *South Park*, Kyle, one of the characters on the show, a loudmouth middle-school student, is trying to make the basketball team at his school. He tries out for the team but ends up not making it because his coach says he lacks the skills and height to be a basketball player. Later in the episode, Kyle comes to find out that his school counselor has changed his gender from being male to female. This leads Kyle to believe that if he changed his race and became black, he would be a better basketball player and thus make the school basketball team.

The episode cleverly plays on society's stereotypes about race and gender identity and addresses the question, if someone can change their gender, why can't someone change their race? It's an interesting point that challenges the notion "Can someone be whoever they want to be."

Some would argue that race is a human construction whereas gender is not. But when determining gender or whether someone is transgender or nonbinary, it does not necessarily come down to genetics but how someone feels.

Being transracial would be offensive to many racial groups because a person that claims to be part of a racial or ethnic group in which they are not part of does not share the history, culture, and experiences of that group. But if you do a DNA test today, science may tell you otherwise, and that you may belong to another racial group or several other racial groups. You may then say to yourself, "I want to identify with my new race." But does that mean you could easily become part of that group or does one need to be accepted by that group?

Most people are gender fluid. When I was growing up there were rockers who put on makeup, wore tight-fitting cloths, and had beautiful long hair. There were kids who emulated them. Some questioned the rockers' gender fluidity and wondered about their sexuality. Gender identity is a process. There are plenty of cases of people airing their gender identity just to get attention. But most people who feel that their bodies do not match with their gender is real.

The *Frontline* documentary "Growing Up Trans" follows several children some who have yet to reach puberty who feel their gender identity does not match their bodies. It is evident in the film that some parents are open and willing to help their child, others need more time, and some are outright defiant. New drugs that essentially block, or at least delay, the onset of puberty is offered to these children to give them and their families more time to make a decision on their transition. The blockers are purely experimental, and no one knows about the long-term effects of them.

In the film, the children are asked to make adult decisions. The parents also struggle, and most worry about their kid's well-being. According to the American Academy of Pediatrics,

> nearly 14% of adolescents reported a previous suicide attempt. Female to male adolescents reported the highest rate of attempted suicide (50.8%), followed by adolescents who identified as not exclusively male or female (41.8%), male to female adolescents (29.9%), questioning adolescents (27.9%), female adolescents (17.6%), and male adolescents (9.8%). Identifying as non-heterosexual exacerbated the risk for all adolescents except for those who did not exclusively identify as male or female (ie, nonbinary). For transgender adolescents, no other sociodemographic characteristic was associated with suicide attempts.[4]

There is undoubtedly today a culture developing around being transgendered or nonbinary. Transgender does not necessarily mean that someone is changing their gender; it can mean that they are not sure and are trying to figure that out for themselves and they need more time. As such, should such a group be categorized as being male or female? Some would say it does matter what people think and how the world views someone and this is what this group is trying to do, to be recognized and acknowledged as a distinct group.

There was a time in the United States it did not matter to many Americans what people did in their personal lives. Even where I grew up, in a mostly working-class community, people knew that all families had to make difficult decisions and it was not for others to judge.

As teachers, we must respect what our students want to be called or how they want to be identified. My official name is Theodore Georgios Zervas, but I tell people to call me Ted. It makes it easy for someone else to learn my name and I don't want to put them in the position of feeling uncomfortable if they pronounced my name incorrectly. But that's just me. Someone else might say they want to be called Theodoros, and that's just fine as well. If I am traveling somewhere else in the world, I sometimes run into a stranger and ask them for directions, I may not speak their language, and they may not speak mine, but we still try to find a way to understand each other. We may find a student on our class roster whose name is Katherine but she tells us she prefers to be called Katy, LaQuesha corrects us and tells us the hyphen is on the last "a" and not the first "a," and Brian prefers to be called Briana with the pronouns she/her/hers or they. It comes down to what the students feel comfortable to be called and not what we want to call them. Our goal is to provide an environment where all our students feel safe and comfortable so learning can happen.

## LEARNING HOW NOT TO FOOL YOUR STUDENTS

Curriculum is almost like scripture. Its main purpose is to help the learner learn the subject. For learning to happen, it must be active and the curriculum must come to life. But learning should also be clear, and students should be given time to process the information and the teacher should never assume that all her students have learned the material.

Take, for example, a story that American physicists Richard Feynman (1918–1988) used to tell his students. During World War II, the U.S. Army built a base on a small island in the South Pacific. The locals on the islands noticed the base. They later saw the Americans building an airfield. Once the airfield was built, they saw planes coming in and landing. The locals became enthralled by all the planes coming in and out from their island.

When the War ended, the Americans decided they would leave, but before they left, they destroyed their base and airfield. The locals continued to watch to see if any planes would continue to land but found that no planes were coming. They figured it was because there wasn't an airfield anymore. So, they attempted to bring back the planes by recreating the same conditions that the Americans created when they first came to the island.

They built a runway, with

fires along the sides of the runways . . . a wooden hut for a man to sit in, with two wooden pieces on his head like headphones and bars of bamboo sticking out like antennas—he [was] the controller—and they [waited] for the airplanes to land.[5]

Just as the Americans had done. After they were finished, they found that there were still no planes. They thought to themselves, "How can that be?" Everything was the same as when the American's were there.

According to Feynman, problems like this continue to puzzle people. But following the same structure does not necessarily produce the same results. The value is found in the *process*, not in the end product. This is what matters in the end in the classroom: "The idea is to try to give all the information to help others to judge . . . not just the information that leads to judgment in one particular direction or another," Feynman noted.[6] I am guilty of this as well when my students were learning about the ancient Olympics Games. I told them that all the athletes competed naked. They were fascinated by this and many had questions. One student asked me,

"So, they played all sports naked?"
I said, "Yes. All sports. Why?"
"You mean they played baseball naked."
"No!" I said, "They did not have basketball then."
"Then did they play baseball naked."
"No, they did not have baseball either."
He shrugged his shoulders to me and said, "Then what sports did they play?"

Our students need to be given all the information before we make assumption on what they know. I assumed all my students knew what sports were being played at the ancient Olympic Games. But they didn't.

## NOTES

1. Spring, Joel. (2015). *American Education.* New York and London: Routledge.
2. Massey, Douglas S. and Denton, Nancy N. (1993). *American Apartheid: Segregation and the Making of the Underclass.* Cambridge, MA: Harvard University Press.
3. Ibid.

4. Toomey, Russell B., Syvertsen, Amy K., and Shramko, Maura. (2018). "Transgender Adolescent Suicide Behavior." *Pediatrics*, 142(4), pp. 1–8.

5. Feynman, R. P. (1974). "Cargo Cult Science: Some Remarks on Science, Pseudoscience, and Learning How Not to Fool Yourself. Cargo Cult Science." Retrieved October 25, 2021, from https://calteches.library.caltech.edu/51/2/CargoCult.htm.

6. Ibid.

# Conclusion

## *The Ideal(ist) Teacher*

Many teachers feel that they can change the world. There is nothing wrong in believing this. I would prefer an idealist teacher over a realist teacher, any day. As teachers we have to see ourselves as something bigger, something more important. It is important for us to know who we are and who are our students. At the same time, we should ask ourselves: Are we contributing to the problem or are we part of the solution? This is a big question. It is an important question. The history of education in the United States is fraught with injustice, discrimination, and violence. As teachers, we are often agents to this, unwittingly or wittingly. The Brazilian philosopher Paolo Freire said:

> No pedagogy which is truly liberating can remain distant from the oppressed by treating them as unfortunates and by presenting for their emulation models from among the oppressors. The oppressed must be their own example in the struggle for their redemption.[1]

Scores of indigenous children gave up their language and culture because of schools. The indigenous scholar Blair Stonechild writes about his experience in Canadian Residential Schools. He says:

> As a youngster, I spent nine years in the Qu'Appelle Indian residential school in the late 1950s and early 1960s. The residential school system was based upon a reformatory model: Indigenous peoples were seen as morally and intellectually deficient, hence education had to be laced with copious amounts of discipline and Christian religious indoctrination. I recall the endless prayers that we were required to utter daily upon rising, going to meals and classes.[2]

Later with mass immigration to the United States in the late nineteenth and early twentieth centuries, immigrant children were trained in schools by teachers to work in factories for low wages in very difficult and unsafe conditions so capitalists could make a lot of money. Black and brown children did not receive an education because it was believed that they did not deserve one or that they were not human enough. Indeed, more needs to be done, and we have not done enough to solve the problems in schools today.

But can a teacher change the world alone? Is it easy for a teacher to get sucked up in all the drama and feel like they are holding the weight of the world on their shoulders? The greatest impact any teacher can have is on her students. A teacher can't lose sight of this, and while she may realize that she cannot change the world, she can truly change her students' lives. This is perhaps one of the greatest impacts that any teacher can have on the world.

Early in this book, I wrote about why Agamemnon, the king of Mycenae, would make a terrible teacher. There are plenty of people like Agamemnon in the world today. We don't need more of them. What we need are teachers who teach students how to be better and how to make the world better.

After Iphigenia is killed, the winds do come back at Aulis and the Greeks set sail for Troy. After ten years of fighting, the Greeks realize that the only way they can win is if they breach the walls of Troy. But the walls of Troy are impenetrable. Legend has it that they were built by the gods themselves and that no army would be able to destroy them. So, the Greeks have to come up with an innovative plan.

One morning, the Greeks hastily load up all their things and pretend to leave. But just before they go, they leave a giant wooden horse outside the walls of Troy. It is their way of saying to the Trojans, "Fine you guys won. We give up. Here is a gift from us to you. See you later." The Trojans see the horse and figure that the Greeks left it as a gift for their victory. An argument erupts on what to do with the horse, but the Trojans decide to bring the horse back into the city. All the while there are several Greeks hiding within the hallows of the giant horse. They sit quietly for night to fall, so they could come out and open the gates to their fellow Greeks outside.

When night finally comes, the Greeks come out and open the gates while the Trojans are still sleeping. What happens next is often left out of the history books. The Greeks enter Troy and go on a killing spree. Young, old, women, men, and children are all killed. Few are spared. Afterward the Greeks loot the city and burn it to the ground. Historians often cite this event as the first recorded act of genocide in human history. It is a heinous act against humanity. What the fall of Troy teaches us is that humans have a propensity to do great harm to one another. It is teachers, however, who teach our students how to be kind, compassionate, and what it means to be a human being. This is why they are important.

The other story that sometimes gets neglected is the story of Odysseus who seeks to find the best teacher for his son, Telemachus, before he leaves for Troy. Odysseus ends up hiring Mentor, who is said to be the greatest teacher in all of Greece. But Odysseus knows it takes more than just a teacher to educate his son. So, Odysseus prays to the goddess Athena for her help. Athena hears his prayers and decides to impart part of her spirit into Mentor. Mentor thus becomes the ultimate teacher. He possesses three important qualities: the astute care of a teacher, the great wisdom of a goddess, and the unconditional love of a parent. It takes more than just the teacher for a child to succeed. Odysseus knew this, as did others during his time.

Today many believe that truth is relative, and that believing is no longer mysterious. We are divided on what should be taught in schools, how it should be taught, and who should teach it. Schools are supposed to bring people and communities together and not divide them, but as Parker Palmer notes:

> The fact that we have schools does not mean we have an education. The fact that we hospitals does not means that we have health care. The fact that we have courts does not mean we have justice. The fact that we have churches, synagogues, and mosques does not mean we have faith.[3]

It is easy for me to point out in this book the problems in teaching and education without offering any solutions. Here are some solutions in helping teachers and students succeed in schools and hopefully solving some of these problems.

- Implement training programs in schools for parents to help their students.
- Teach empathy to students.
- Conduct teacher swap programs/sabbatical leaves for teachers.
- Focus on social-emotional learning and the entire child.
- Implement more vocational programs in schools and get rid of the stigma of these programs.
- Invest in the arts. They do have many benefits to students.
- Help students find their talents and then help them cultivate those talents.
- Don't change for the sake of change.
- Believe in a self-fulfilling prophecy for your students. It does work.
- Involve all stakeholders and help teachers take ownership.
- Decentralize large school systems and deal with corruption before it gets worse.
- Change the way we think about teachers like in Finland, South Korea, and Singapore.

- Don't just focus on the teachers and the school but on the community as well.
- Understand that because it works at one school doesn't mean it will work at another school.
- Remember the saying, "it does take a village."

## NOTES

1. Freire, Paulo. (2009). *Pedagogy of the Oppressed.* New York: The Continuum International Publishing Group, p. 54.

2. Stonechild, Blair. (forthcoming). "Revitalizing Indigenous Belief Systems: Implications for Curriculum." In Abdou, Ehaab D. and Zervas, Theodore G. (eds.), *Reconciling Ancient and Indigenous Belief Systems: Textbooks and Curricula in Contention.* Toronto, CA: University of Toronto Press.

3. Parker, Palmer. (2007). *The Courage to Teach: Exploring the Inner Landscape of a Teacher's Life.* San Francisco, CA: John Wiley & Sons, p. 204.

# Selected Bibliography

I consulted with several sources for this book. Many of had read and some I have used in my courses. The works listed below are books and articles that have helped me complete this book, all of which I recommend to you.

Adams, Wallace David. (1995). *Education for Extinction: American Indians and the Boarding School Experience, 1875-1928.* Missouri, KS: University of Kansas Press.

Akhtar, Ayad. (2020). *Homeland Elegies: A Novel.* New York: Little, Brown and Company.

Allensworth, Elaine et al. (2009). "The School Teachers Leave: Teacher Mobility in Chicago Public Schools." *University of Chicago Consortium of School Research.*

American Psychological Association. (2015). *APA Review Confirms Link Between Playing Violent Video Games and Aggression.* http://www.apa.org/news/press/releases/2015/08/violent-video-games.aspx

Andrews, Arin. (2015). *Some Assembly Required. The Not-So-Secret Life of a Transgender Teen.* New York: Simon & Schuster.

Antin, May. (1912). *The Promised Land.* Boston, MA and New York: Houghton Mifflin Company.

Anyon, Jean. (1997). *Ghetto Schooling: A Political Economy of Urban Educational Reform.* New York and London: Teachers College Press.

Appiah, Kwame Anthony. (2006). *Cosmopolitanism: Ethics in a World of Strangers.* New York and London: W.W. Norton & Company.

———. (2010). *The Honor Code: How Moral Revolutions Happen.* New York and London: W.W. Norton & Company.

Apple, Michael W., ed. (2003). *The State and the Politics of Knowledge.* New York: Routledge Farmer.

Apple, Michael W. and Christian-Smith, Linda K., eds. (1991). *The Politics of the Textbook.* New York: Routledge.

Aries, Philippe. (1962). *Centuries of Childhood: A Social History of Family Life.* New York: Vintage Books.

Ayers, William et al., ed. (2008). *City Kids, City Schools: More Reports from the Front Row.* New York and London: New Press.

Barnard, Henry, ed. (1861). *Memoirs of Educators.* New York: F.C. Brownell.

Barone, Tom. (2001). *Touching Eternity: The enduring Outcomes of Teaching.* New York and London: Teachers College Press.

Barry, Kathleen. (2000). *Susan B. Anthony: A Biography of a Singular Feminist.* Bloomington, IN: 1st Book Library.

Bayoumi, Moustpha. (2009). *How it Feels to Be a Problem: Being Young and Arab in America.* London, UK: Penguin books.

Beecher, Catherine. (1846). The Evils Suffered by American Women and American Children: The Causes and *the Remedy/Presented in an Address by C.E. Beecher, to Meetings of Ladies in Cincinnati, Washington, Baltimore, Philadelphia, New York, and Other Cities. Also, An Address to the Protestant Clergy of the United States.* New York: Harper & Brothers.

———. (2016). *The Duty of American Women to Their Country.* Palala Press.

Bernal, Martin. (1987). *Black Athena: The Afroasiatic Roots of Classical Civilization.* New Brunswick, NJ: Rutgers University Press.

Berrol, Selma Contor. (1993). *Julia Richman: A Nobel Woman.* Philadelphia, PA: Balch Institute for Ethnic Studies.

Bloom, Alan. (1987). *The Closing of the American Mind.* New York: Simon and Shuster.

Bloom, Benjamin S. et al. (1956). *Taxonomy of Educational Objectives: The Classification of Educational Goals.* Longman, WI: Longmans, Green & Co Ltd.

Bodnar, John. (1987). *The Transplanted: A History of Immigrants in Urban America.* Bloomington, IN: Indiana University Press.

Brackett, Marc. (2019). *Permission to Feel: Unlocking the Power of Emotions to Help our Kids, Ourselves, and Our Society Thrive.* Celadon Books.

Brook, Gary. (2019). *Go See the Principal: True Tales From the School Trenches.* Da Capo Lifelong Books.

Brown, Brené. (2015). *Daring Greatly: How the Courage to Be Vulnerable Transforms the Way We Live, Love, Parent, and Lead.* New York: Avery.

Buckley, Madeline. (2017). "Nearly 3,000 People Shot in Chicago So Far this Year." *Chicago Tribune.*

Burns, J.A. (1910). *The Growth and Development of the Catholic School System in the United States.* New York and Cincinnati: Benzinger Brothers.

Burstyn, Joan N. (1974). "Catharine Beecher and the Education of American Women." *The New England Quarterly,* 47(3), pp. 386–403.

Butchart, Ronald E. (2010). *Schooling and the Freed People: Teaching, Learning, and the Struggle for Black Freedom, 1861-1876.* Chapel Hill, NC: University of North Carolina Press.

Capo Crucet, Jeannine. (2016). *Make Your Home Among Strangers.* London, UK: Picador Press.

Carver-Thomas, Desiree and Darling-Hammond, Linda. (2017). "Teacher Turnover and Why it Matter? What we can do About it." *Learning Policy Institute.*

Center for Research on Educational Outcomes (CREDO). (2013). *National Charter School Study.* Stanford, CA: Stanford University.

Cimbala, Paul A. and Miller, Randal M, ed. (1999). *The Freedmen's Bureau and Reconstruction: Reconsiderations.* New York: Fordham University Press.

Cisneros, Sandra. (2016). *A House of My Own: Stories From My Life.* New York: Vintage.

Coats, Ta-Nehisi. (2015). *Between the World and Me.* New York: Spiegel & Grau.

Codell, Esme Raji. (1999). *Education Esme: Diary of a Teacher's First Year.* New York: Algonquin Books of Chapel Hill.

Conley, Garrard. (2016). *Boy Erased: A Memoir.* New York: Riverhead Books.

Connolly, Daniel. (2016). *The Book of Isaias: A Child of Hispanic Immigrants Seeks His Own America.* New York: St. Martin's Press.

Coppin, Fanny. (1913). *Reminiscences of School Life, and Hints on Teaching.* Philadelphia, Pennsylvania. African Methodist Episcopal Book Concern.

Cott, Nancy F. (1997). *The Bonds of Womanhood: Women's Sphere in England, 1780-1835.* New Haven, CT: Yale University Press.

Critchley, Simon. (2019). *Tragedy, the Greeks, and Us.* New York: Vintage.

Danielson, Charlotte. (2007). *Enhancing Professional Practice: A Framework for Teaching.* Alexandria, VA: Association for Supervision & Curriculum Development.

Darling-Hammond, Linda. (2006). *Powerful Teacher Education: Lessons From Exemplary Programs.* San Francisco, CA: Jossey Bass.

―――. (2010). *The Flat World and Education: How America's Commitment to Equity Will Determine Our Future.* New York: Teacher College Press.

Darling-Hammond, Linda and Bransford, John ed. (2005). *Preparing Teachers for A Changing World: What Teachers Should Learn and Be Able to Do.* San Francisco, CA: Jossey Bass.

Darling-Hammond, Linda, et al. (2017). *Empowered Educators: How High-Performing Systems Shape Teaching Quality Around the World.* San Francisco, CA: Jossey-Bass.

Davis, Joshua. (2014). *Spare Parts. Four Undocumented Teenagers, One Ugly Robot and the Battle for the American Dream.* New York: FSG Originals.

Dawson, Juno. (2015). *This Book is Gay.* New York: Sourcebook Fire.

Delpit, Lisa ed. (2019). *Teaching When the World is on Fire: Authentic Classroom Advice, from Climate Justice to Black Lives Matter.* New York and London: The New Press.

Department of Education. (1870). *Report of the Commissioner of Education on the Improvement of Public Schools in the District of Columbia.* Washington, DC: Government Printing Office.

Dewey, John. (1916). *Democracy and Education.* New York: The Free Press.

―――. (1938). *John Dewey Experience and Education.* New York: Simon & Shuster.

Diamond, Jared. (2017). *Guns, Germs, and Steel: The Fates of Human Societies.* New York: W.W. Norton & Company.

Douty, Esther Morris. (1971). *Charlotte Forten, Free Black Teacher.* New York: Garrard Publishing Co.

Dubois, W.E.B. (1901). *The Negro Common School.* Atlanta, GA: University Press.

———. (2002). *The Education of Black People: Ten Critiques, 1906-1960.* New York: Monthly Review Press.

Duncan, Arne. (2018). *How Schools Work: An Inside Account of Failure and Success from One of the Nation's Longest-Serving Secretaries of Education.* New York: Simon & Shuster.

Emdin, Christopher. (2016). *For White Folks Who Teach in the Hood...And the Rest of Y'all Too: reality Pedagogy and Urban Education.* Boston, MA: Beacon Press.

Emmanuel, Nelson S, ed. (2000). *African American Authors, 1745-1945: A Biographical and Critical Sourcebook.* Westport, CT and London: Greenwood Press.

Fairbanks, Mary Mason. (1898). *Emma Willard and Her Pupils or Fifty Years of Troy Female Seminary, 1822-1872.* New York: Mrs. Russell Sage Publications.

Fass, Paula S. (1989). *Outside In: Minorities and the Transformation of American Education.* London and New York. Oxford University Press.

Feinberg, Walter and Soltis, Jonas F. (2004). *School and Society.* New York: Teachers College Press.

Forten, Charlotte. (1864). "Life on the Sea Islands." *Atlantic Monthly.* https://www.theatlantic.com/magazine/archive/1864/05/life-on-the-sea-islands/308758/

———. (1981). *The Journal of Charlotte L. Forten: A Free Negro in the Slave Era.* New York: W.W. Norton & Company.

Foucault, Michel. (1979). *Discipline & Punish: The Birth of the Prison.* New York: Vintage.

Fowler, William Worthington. (2015). *Woman on the American Frontier: A Valuable and Authentic History of the Heroism, Adventures, Privations, Captivities, Trials, and Noble Lives and Deaths of the Pioneer Mothers of the Republic.* Springville, UT: Repressed Publishing.

Freire, Paulo. (2009). *Pedagogy of the Oppressed.* New York: The Continuum International Publishing Group.

Friedman, Hannah. (2009). *Everything Sucks: Losing My Mind and Finding Myself in a High School Quest for Cool.* Boca, Raton, FL: HCI Teens.

Gaither, Milton. (2017). *Homeschool an American History.* New York and London: Palgrave & Macmillan.

Gates, Henry Louis and Higginbotham, Evelyn Brooks, ed. (2004). *African American Lives.* London and New York: Oxford University Press.

Gentile, Douglas A. et al. (2017). "Violent Video Games on Salivary Cortisol, Arousal, and Aggressive Thoughts in Children." *Computers in Human Behavior.*

Gillam, Victor, F. (1890). "The Inevitable Result to the American Workingman of Unrestricted Immigration." Chromolithograph. *Judge.*

Gilliam, Walter S. "Early Childhood Expulsions and Suspensions Undermining Our Nation's Most Promising Agent of Opportunity and Social Justice." Robert Wood Johnson Foundation.

Giroux, Henry A. (1997). *Pedagogy and the Politics of Hope: Theory, Culture and Schooling, A Reader.* Boulder, CO: Westview Press.

Goldstein, Dana. (2014). *Teacher Wars: A History of America's Most Embattled Profession.* New York: Anchor Books.

Goodsell, Willystine. (1970). *Pioneers of Women's Education in the United States: Emma Willard, Catherine Beecher, Mary Lyon.* New York: AMS Press.

Graber, Kay ed. (2004). *Sister to the Sioux: The Memoirs of Elaine Goodale Eastman 1885- 1891.* Lincoln, NE: University of Nebraska Press.

Gradel, Thomas J., Simpson, Dick, and Zenellis, Andris. (2008). "Curing Corruption in Illinois: Anti-Corruption Report Number 1." Unpublished. University of Illinois at Chicago Department of Political Science.

Green, Elizabeth. (2014). *Building a Better Teacher: How Teaching Works and How to Teach it to Everyone.* New York and London: W.W Norton & Company.

Greene, Maxine. (1995). *Releasing the Imagination: Essays on Education, the Arts and Social Change.* San Francisco, CA: Jossey Bass.

Greene, Ross W. (2014). *Lost at School: Why Our Kids with Behavioral Challenges are Falling Through the Cracks and How We Can Help Them.* London, New York, Toronto, Sydney and New Delhi: Scriber.

Greenfield, Susan. (2015). *Mind Change: How Digital Technologies Are Leaving Their Mark on Our Brains.* New York: Random House.

Gutek, Gerald L. (1972). *A History of the Western Educational Experience.* Long Grove, IL: Waveland Press.

Haley, Margaret. (1904). "Why Teachers Should Organize." *Journal of Education,* 60(18), pp. 145–152.

Hansen, David T. (1995). *The Call To Teach.* New York: Teachers College Press.

Haroutunian-Gordon, Sophie. (1991). *Turning the Soul: Teaching Through Conversation in the High School.* Chicago and London: University of Chicago Press.

———. (2009). *Learning Through Discussion: The Art of Turning the Soul.* New Haven and London: Yale University Press.

Harrison, Robert. (2011). *Washington During Civil War and Reconstruction: Race and Radicalism.* Cambridge and New York. Cambridge University Press.

Havighurst, Robert J. (1964). *The Public Schools of Chicago: A Survey for the Board of Education of the City of Chicago.* Chicago, IL: The Board of Education of the City of Chicago.

Hinduja, Sameer & Patchin, Justin W. (2010). "Bullying, Cyberbullying, and Suicide." *Archives of Suicide Research,* 14(3), pp. 206–221.

Hoffman, Nancy. (1981). *Woman's True Profession: Voices from the History of Teaching.* New York: The Feminist Press.

Jones, LeAlan and Newman, Lloyd. (1998). *Our America: Life and Death in the South Side of Chicago.* New York: Scribner.

Kaluf, Kevin, J. and Rogers, George E. (2011). "The Gary Plan: A Model for Today's Education?" *Journal of STWM Teacher Education,* 48(1), pp. 13–21.

Kendi, Ibram X. (2016). *Stamped From the Beginning: The Definitive History of Racists Ideas in America.* New York: Bold Type.

———. (2019). *How to Be An Antiracists.* New York: One World.

Kliebard, Herbert M. (1986). *The Struggle for the American Curriculum: 1893-1958.* New York: Routledge & Kegan Paul.

Kozol, Jonathan. (1991). *Savage Inequalities: Children in America's Schools.* New York: Crown.

————. (2005). *The Shame of the Nation: Restoration of Apartheid Schooling in America.* New York: Three Rivers Press.

Ladson-Billings, Gloria. (2009). *The Dreamkeepers: Successful Teachers of African American Children.* San Francisco, CA: Jossey-Bass.

Leavitt, Steven D and Dubner, Stephen J. (2009). *Freakonomics: A Rogue Economists The Hidden Side of Everything.* New York: William Murrow Paperbacks.

Lemov, Doug. (2010). *Teach Like a Champion 2.0: 62 Techniques that Put Students to the Path of College.* San Francisco, CA: Jossey-Bass.

Loewen, James W. (1996). *Lies My Teacher Told Me: Everything Your American History Textbook Got Wrong.* New York: Touchstone.

Lord, J. (1873). *The Life of Emma Willard.* New York: D. Appleton and Co.

Loughran, John and Russell Tom ed. (1997). *Teaching about Teaching: Purpose Passion and Pedagogy in Teacher Education.* London & New York. Routledge Falmer.

Lynd, Albert. (1953). *Quackery in Public Schools.* New York: Little, Brown & Company.

Mabee, Carleton. (1968). "A Negro Boycott to Integrate Boston Schools." *New England Quarterly,* 41(3), pp. 341–361.

Mann, Horace. (2010). *Life and Works of Horace MANN, Vol 3.* Charleston, SC. Nabu Press.

Massey, Douglas S. and Denton, Nancy N. (1993). *American Apartheid: Segregation and the Making of the Underclass.* Cambridge, MA: Harvard University Press.

May, Vivian M. (2012). *Anna Julia Cooper, Visionary Black Feminist: A Critical Introduction.* New York and London: Routledge.

Maynard, Nathan and Weinstein, Brad. (2019). *Hacking School Discipline: 9 Ways to Create a Culture of Empathy and Responsibility Using Restorative Justice.* Times 10 Publications.

McCourt, Frank. (2005). *Teacher Man.* London, New York, Toronto, Sydney and New Delhi: Scriber.

Michie, Gregory. (2009). *Holler if You Can Hear Me: The Education of a Teacher and His Students.* New York: Teachers College Press.

Miller, Alice. (1996). *The Drama of the Gifted Child: The Search of the True Self.* New York: Basic Books.

Moghul, Haroon. (2017). *How to Be a Muslim: An American Story.* Boston, MA: Beacon Press.

Mondale, Sarah and Patton, Sarah B., ed. (2001). *School: The Story of American Public Education.* Boston, MA: Beacon Press.

Moore, Wes. (2010). *The Other Wes Moore: One Name Two Fates.* New York: One World.

National Education Association of the United States. (1918). *Cardinal Principles of Secondary Education. A Report of the Commission on the Reorganization of Secondary Education appointed by the National Education Association.* Bulletin No. 5.

Nietz, John A. *The Evolution of American Secondary School Textbook.* Rutland, VT: Charles E. Tuttle Company.

Nussbaum, Martha C. (1997). *Cultivating Humanity: A Classical Defense of Reform in Liberal Education.* Cambridge, MA: Harvard University Press.

———. (2013). *Creating Capabilities: The Human Development Approach.* Cambridge, MA: Harvard University Press.

Orange, Tommy. (2019). *There There.* New York: Vintage.

Palmer, Parker J. (2007). The Courage to Teach: Exploring the Inner Landscape of a Teacher's Life. Hoboken, NJ: John Wiley & Sons.

Patel, Eboo. (2010). *Acts of Faith: The Story of an American Muslim in the Struggle of a Soul of a Generation.* Boston, MA: Beacon Press.

PBS/Frontline. (2016). *The Education of Omarina.* https://www.pbs.org/video/frontline-education-omarina/

Perkins, Linda Mary. (1978). *Fanny Jackson Coppin and the Institute for Colored Youth: A Model of Nineteenth Century Black Female Educational and Community Leadership, 1837-1902.* Unpublished Dissertation. Urbana-Champaign, IL: University of Illinois at Urbana-Champaign.

———. (1983). "The Impact of the Cult of True Woman Hood on Black Women." *Journal of Social Issues,* 39(3), pp. 17–28.

Piaget, Jean. (1997). *The Moral Judgement of the Child.* New York and London: Free Press Paperbacks.

Plato. (1953). *The Republic.* New York: Penguin Books.

———. (1956). *Protagoras and Meno.* New York: Penguin Books.

Pollizer, William S. (1999). *The Gullah People and Their African Heritage.* Athens, GA. University of Georgia Press.

Ravitch, Diane. (2014). *Reign of Error: The Hoax of the Privatization Movemennet and the Danger to America's Public Schools.* New York: Alfred A. Knopf.

Reese, William J. (2005). *America's Public Schools: From the Common School to "No Child Left Behind."* Baltimore, MD: John Hopkins University Press.

Reeves, Ellen Gordon, ed. (2006). *The New Press Education Reader: Leading Educators Speak Out.* New York and London: New Press.

Reid, Robert L. (1982). *Battleground the Autobiography of Margaret Haley.* Chicago, Il. University of Illinois Press.

Renner, Marguerite. (1981). *Who Will Teach? Changing Job Opportunity and Roles for Women in the Evolution of the Pittsburgh Public Schools, 1830-1900.* Unpublished Dissertation. Pittsburgh, PA: University of Pittsburgh.

Repousis, Angelo. (2004). "The Trojan Women: Emma Hart Willard and the Troy Society for the Advancement of Female Education in Greece." *Journal of the Early Republic,* 24(3), pp. 445–476.

Rhodes, Jean E. et al. (2000). "Agents of Change: Pathways Through Which Mentoring Relationships Influence Adolescents' Academic Adjustment." *Child Development.*

Richman, Julia. (1905). "The Immigrant Child." In *Journal of Proceedings and Addresses of the Forty-Fourth Annual Meeting.* Winona, MN: National Educational Association, p. 113.

Robinson, Ken and Aronica, Lou. (2014). *Finding Your Element. How to Discover Your Talents and Passions and Transform your Life.* London and New York. Penguin books.

Rousmaniere, Kate. (2005). *Citizen Teacher: The Life and Leadership of Margaret Haley.* Albany, NY: State University New York Press.

Rury, John, ed. (2005). *Urban Education in the United States: A Historical Reader.* New York: Palgrave Macmillan.

———. (2019). *Education and Social Change: Contours in the History of American Schooling.* New York: Routledge.

———. (2020). *Creating the Suburban School Advantage: Race, Localism, and Inequality in an American Metropolis.* Ithaca, NY: Cornell University Press.

Sadovnik, Alan R. et al. (2013). *Exploring Education: An Introduction to the Foundations of Education.* New York and London: Routledge.

Sahlberg, Pasi. (2015). *Finish Lessons 2.0: What Can the World Learn from Educational Change in Finland?* New York: Teachers College Press.

Said, Edward. *Orientalism.* (1980). London and New York. Routledge & Kegan Paul.

Saloutos, Theodore. (1956). *They Remember America: The Story of Repatriated Greek Americans.* Los Angeles, CA: University of California Press.

Santiago, Esmerelda. (2006). *When I was Puerto Rican: A Memoir.* New York: Da Capo Press.

Santoro, Doris. (2018). Demoralized: Why Teachers Leave the Profession They Love and How They Can Stay. Cambridge, MA: Harvard University Press.

Schissler, Hanna and Soysal, Yasemin Nuhoglu, eds. (2005). *The Nation Europe and the World: Textbooks and Curricula in Transition.* New York: Berghahn Books.

Shaw, Ann Marie. (1903). "The True Character of New York Public Schools." *World Works*, 7(2), p. 4206.

Shorto, Russell. (2010). "How Christian Were the Founders? History Wars: Inside America's Textbook Battles." *The New York Times Magazine*, pp. 32–39.

Sini, Rozina. (April, 2017). "You are Being Programmed, Former Facebook Executive Warns." *BBC News.* http://www.bbc.com/news/blogs-trending -42322746 Retrieved April 18, 2018.

Skloot, Rebecca. (2011). *The Immortal Life of Harriette Lacks.* New York: Crown.

Slaughter, Diana T, ed. (1988). *Black Children and Poverty: A Developmental Perspective.* San Francisco, CA: Jossey-Bass.

Smith, Eric Ledell. (2003). "To Teach My People: Fanny Jackson Coppin and Philadelphia's Institute for Colored Youth." *Pennsylvania Heritage, 29*(1), pp. 6–11.

Smith, Glen L. and Smith Joan K, ed. (1999). *Lives in Education: A Narrative of People and Ideas.* Mahwah, NJ: Lawrence Erlbaum Publishers.

Snyder, Thomas D, ed. (1993). *120 Years of American Education: A Statistical Portrait.* Washington, DC: National Center of Educational Statistics.

Soumakis, Fevronia and Zervas, Theodore G, ed. (2020). *Educating Greek Americans: Historical and Contemporary Pathways.* New York and London: Palgrave and Macmillan.

Spring, Joel. (2015). *American Education.* New York and London: Routledge.

Stanley, G. Hall. (1906). *Youth its Education, Regimen, and Hygiene.* New York: D. Appleton and Company.

Steinbeck, John. (2003). *East of Eden.* New York: Viking Press.

Stockdale, Laura A. et al. (2015). "Emotionally Anesthetized: Media Violence Induces Neural Changes During Emotional Face Processing." *Social Cognitive and Affective Neuroscience.*

Talmi, Debra. (2013). "Enhanced Emotional Memory: Cognitive and Neural Mechanisms." *Current Directions in Psychological Sciences,* 22(6), pp. 430–436.

Taylor, Kay Ann. (2005). "Mary S. Peake and Charlotte L. Forten: Black Teachers During the Civil War Reconstruction." *The Journal of Negro Education,* 74(2), pp. 124–137.

Thorburn, Michael. (2017). "John Dewey, William Wirt and the Gary Schools Plan: A Centennial Reappraisal." *Journal of Educational Administration and History,* 2(49), pp. 144–156.

Thorndike, Edward Lee. (1904). *An Introduction to the Theory of Mental and Social Measurements.* New York: The Science Press.

———. (1906). *The Principles of Teaching Based on Psychology.* Syracuse: The Mason-Henry Press.

Tough, Paul. (2009). *Whatever it Takes: Geoffrey Canada's Quest to Change Harlem and America.* New York: Mariner Books.

Tozer, Steven E. et al. (1998). *School and Society: Historical and Contemporary Perspective.* New York: McGraw-Hill Education.

Turner, Frederick Jackson. (2016). *The Frontier in American History.* Palala Press.

Turpin, Andrea L. (2010). "The Ideological Origins of the Women's College: Religion, Class and Curriculum in the Educational Visions of Catharine Beecher and Mary Lyon." *History of Education Quarterly,* 50(2), pp. 133–158.

Tyack, David and Cuban, Larry. (1995). *Tinkering toward Utopia: A Century of Public School Reform.* Cambridge, MA: Harvard University Press.

Tyack, David and Hansot, Elizabeth. (1992). *Learning Together: A History of Coeducation in American Public Schools.* New York: Russell Sage Foundation.

Tyler, Ralph R. (1949). *Basic Principles of Curriculum and Instruction.* Chicago and London: University of Chicago Press.

U.S. Census Bureau. (1918). *Negro Population in the United States, 1790-1915.* Washington, DC: Government Printing.

U.S. Department of Education. National Center of Education Statistics. Washington, DC: Government Printing. https://nces.ed.gov/fastfacts/display.asp?id=28

U.S. Department of Education. National Center of Education Statistics. Washington, DC: Government Printing. https://nces.ed.gov/pubs2016/2016131.pdf

Vinovskis, Maris, A. and Bernard, Richard M. (1978). "Beyond Catharine Beecher: Female Education in the Antebellum Period." *Signs,* 3(4), pp. 856–869.

Vygotsky, Lev. (1997). *Thought and Language.* Cambridge, MA: MIT University Press.

Warren, Donald, ed. (1989). *American Teachers: Histories of a Profession at Work.* New York: Macmillan Publishing Company.

Washington, Booker T. (1995). *Up From Slavery.* Mineola, NY: Dover Publications.

Watson, John B. (1924). *Behaviorism.* New York: W.W. Norton & Company.

Wechler, Alan. (2017). "The International School Surge." *The Atlantic.*

Wei, Susan. (2001). "Reflections of a First-Year Teacher: Learning How to Make a Difference." https://www.edutopia.org/reflections-first-year-teacher

Westover, Tara. (2018) *Educated: A Memoir.* New York: Random House.

Whitehead, Alfred North. (1929). *The Aims of Education and Other Essays.* New York: The Free Press.

Wilkerson, Isabel. (2020). *Caste: The Origins of Discontents.* New York: Random House.

William Seward. (1840). "Annual Message to the Legislature." Reprinted in Baker, *Supra Note* 168, pp. 212–213.

Williams, Thomas Chatterton. (2011). *Loosing My Cool: Love, Literature and a Black Man's Escape from the Crowd.* New York: Penguin Books.

Wilson, Gary. (2014). *Your Brain on Porn: Internet Pornography and the Emerging Science of Addiction.* Kent, UK: Commonwealth Publishing.

Wilson, William Julius. (1987). *The Truly Disadvantaged: The Inner City, the Underclass, and Public Policy.* Chicago and London: University of Chicago Press.

Young, Robert, J.C. (1990). *White Mythologies.* London and New York. Routledge.

Younis, James and Yates Miranda. (1997). *Community Service and Social Responsibility in Youth.* Chicago and London: University of Chicago Press.

Zervas, Theodore G. (2017). "Finding a Balance in Education: Immigration, Diversity, and Schooling in Urban America, 1890-1900." *Athens Journal of Education,* 4(1), pp. 77–84.

Zimmerman, Jonathan. (2002). *Whose America? Culture Wars in the Public Schools.* Cambridge, MA: Harvard University Press.

———. (2015). *Too Hot to Handle: A Global History of Sex Education.* Princeton, NJ and Oxford: Princeton University Press.

———. (2017). *The Case of Contention. Teaching Controversial Issues in American Schools.* Chicago and London: University of Chicago Press.

———. (2020). "Video Kills the Teaching Star: Remote Learning and the Death of Charisma." *The Chronicle of Higher Education.* https://www.chronicle.com/article/video-kills-the-teaching-star/

Zinn, Howard. (1999). *A People's History of the United States.* New York: Harper Perennial Modern Classics.

# Index

# About the Author

**Theodore (Ted) G. Zervas**, PhD, is professor of education and MAT coordinator at North Park University in Chicago. He has taught at Chicago Public Schools, Technologico Superiores De Monterrey in Mexico and The American University in Cairo, Egypt. He is the author of several books and articles on education. He is currently working on an edited book with Ehaab D. Abdou titled *Reconciling Ancient and Indigenous Belief Systems: Textbooks and Curricula in Contention*, which looks at how modern nations from around the world treat their ancient pagan histories in their national textbooks and curricula.

Made in the USA
Monee, IL
02 September 2022

13096762R00090